Industrial Policy and Semiconductors

Industrial Policy and Semiconductors

Missing the Target

Andrew Dick

The AEI Press

Publisher for the American Enterprise Institute

WASHINGTON, D. C.

1995

AEI is grateful to the Sloan Foundation and to the Sasakawa Peace Foundation for their generous support for this project.

Available in the United States from the AEI Press, c/o Publisher Resources Inc., 1224 Heil Quaker Blvd., P.O. Box 7001, La Vergne, TN 37086-7001. Distributed outside the United States by arrangement with Eurospan, 3 Henrietta Street, London WC2E 8LU England.

ISBN 0-8447-7055-8
ISBN 0-8447-7043-4(pbk.)

1 3 5 7 9 10 8 6 4 2

THE AEI PRESS
Publisher for the American Enterprise Institute
1150 17th Street, N.W., Washington, D.C. 20036

Printed in the United States of America

Contents

1
Introduction

One of the most enduring economic lessons from history is that a policy of free, unfettered trade raises countries' standard of living and expands their opportunities for economic growth. Sometimes policy makers have heeded this lesson; other times they have not. Protectionist policies lengthened and deepened the Great Depression in the 1930s. Seeking to protect jobs at home, the United States raised its tariff (tax) on imports by 50 percent, and Europe quickly retaliated by closing its markets to American exports. Literally overnight, markets for factory goods vanished, and unemployment soared to more than 30 percent as plants were idled and companies were forced to lay off employees. Prosperity did not return until a decade later when preparations for World War II boosted national economies.

The 1950s and 1960s, by comparison, represented an era of relative policy enlightenment. The United States and its trading partners slashed import tariffs to less than one-tenth of their postwar level, and liberalization ushered in unparalleled economic growth and prosperity worldwide. Firms expanded production and hired additional employees to meet increased demand at home and abroad. Prices paid by consumers fell, and their incomes grew nearly 5 percent a year over this period, a rate that has remained unmatched since. The 1970s saw the pendulum swing back, as industrial countries once again raised trade barriers and industrial policies grew more interventionist. Increased protection slowed growth in world trade to just one-third

1

of its former rate, and because trade is a primary engine of economic growth, world incomes grew only one-half as quickly as in the two previous decades.[1] The combination of high unemployment and high inflation also led to a new phenomenon: stagflation.

In the 1980s, industrialized countries usually resisted temptations to intervene in the world marketplace. There were notable exceptions, however, when governments that preached the virtues of free trade sometimes found themselves actively managing markets and picking winners and losers. The semiconductor industry, whose story of policy activism is reviewed in detail in this volume, was a notable— and highly costly—experiment in managed-trade policy. As the decade progressed, protectionist exceptions grew more numerous as countries attempted to second-guess the private market by "targeting" favored industries with aggressive industrial and protectionist trade policies. With time, targeting has developed broad support among politicians and journalists. Furthermore, many business firms— those who would be the guinea pigs in future industrial targeting experiments—have also voiced support for interventionist trade and industrial policies.

Targeting has received widespread support because the arguments offered by policy activists have gone largely unchallenged. As a result, there is a common perception among the public at large, and within many policy circles, that targeting successes greatly outnumber failures. Indeed, enthusiasm for targeting appears to be matched only by the equally enthusiastically held belief that *other* countries are always more successful at targeting than one's own government is. Both perceptions are incorrect. In industry after industry—whether in the United States, Western Europe, or Asia—government policies to target favored industries have been costly failures.

The process is virtually the same in each case. A politically vocal industry demands and receives subsidies or favorable tax treatment on the grounds that it is "strategic" to the nation's economy. In most cases, the industry also argues successfully for high barriers to imports to offset the effects of what it perceives as "unfair" foreign competition. Shielded from foreign competition and no longer forced to survive on their own merits, the targeted firms become less productive, their costs rise, their technology grows obsolete, and domestic consumers end up paying for this inefficiency in the form of rising prices, inferior products, and higher taxes to cover steadily growing subsidies to the firms.

Particular targeted industries may *appear* to be successful because the firms continue producing and employees remain in their jobs. But these are the wrong measures for evaluating the track record of targeting. To be judged a success, targeting must meet three stringent tests:

• First, the targeted industry must have grown faster, become more profitable, and generated more employment than the industry would have *without* targeting. Put differently, it is not enough for governments simply to *pick* winners—they must *make* winners.

• Second, any gains received by the targeted firms must outweigh the costs imposed on consumers, who will pay higher prices, and on taxpayers, who will finance the government subsidies.

• Third, and perhaps most important, the correct measure of success is not whether targeting "worked" in a particular sector. Throwing enough government dollars at enough industries is virtually guaranteed to produce at least a few individual "successes." Rather, what matters is whether the policy of targeting leads to higher growth, profits, and employment in the economy as a whole. Targeting must divert capital and labor resources away from some industries to bolster others. If these redirected resources would have earned a higher rate of return in their original use, then targeting has actually lowered the economy's return on its total portfolio of industries.

In practice, targeting most often fails at least one of these three crucial tests. This volume critically evaluates current proposals to target industries with trade and industrial policies. It begins by explaining why proponents' arguments make sense only in *theory*—giving them a superficial appeal—and why in *practice* targeting has led to a string of costly failures. Proponents argue that governments could bolster their firms' international competitive position through subsidies to raise profits, enter new markets, invest in research, and preserve domestic employment. Careful examination shows that targeting has failed to meet any of these goals in the past because private markets have outsmarted government bureaucrats as firms, investors, and consumers have found ways to circumvent the distorting effects of government intervention in a competitive world market. Furthermore, contrary to popular wisdom, targeting's track record has been equally disappointing in Japan and South Korea, two countries that are frequently cited as examples of industrial policy successes. The growth of these economies stems more from entrepreneurial saving and investment than from government policy directives.

The second half of this volume reviews the performance of targeting in the semiconductor industry. Policy activists have claimed that the semiconductor industry is the exception to the rule that targeting does not work and that aggressive trade and industrial policies have actually boosted national incomes and employment in the industry. This analysis carefully evaluates the rationales offered for targeting the semiconductor industry and explores the question of whether any of those rationales have been justified in practice. It finds that targeting is just as unimpressive in semiconductors as in other sectors. The industry is littered with policies whose actual consequences were quite different—and typically much costlier—than targeting proponents promised.

2
Why Has Targeting Gained an Audience?

Ignoring clear economic lessons from history, targeting proponents argue that governments can respond better than private firms to the competitive challenges arising in a global economy. Senior officials in the Clinton administration contend that "American companies [should] get the kind of help from the U.S. government that virtually every other nation gives its business."[1] The same view is widely held among corporate managers. A recent poll of American business managers, for example, found that three-fourths believed the government should "actively help" corporations doing business overseas, and two-thirds argued that the United States should seek to copy Japanese trade and industrial policies.

Why has targeting gained such a receptive audience? Throughout history, public opinion and public policy have been closely tied to popular perceptions of our economic well-being. As a general rule of thumb, the stronger a country's economic health is, the quieter the calls for "protecting jobs and industries" are. During economic downturns, those calls become louder and finally prove irresistible to policy makers. The highly protectionist Smoot-Hawley tariff levied by the United States in 1930, for example, was a reaction to the start of a worldwide economic downturn. American industries demanded protection from foreign competition when they saw their overseas markets erode. With the benefit of hindsight, it is clear that policy makers overreacted and that the Great Depression was deepened and lengthened by widespread protectionism.

In the immediate postwar period, protectionist calls proved irresistible to many developing countries, which believed that a sheltered home market was essential to allow their young industries to mature and prosper. These countries adopted highly protectionist and interventionist policies to nurture their "infant industries." Another common belief among developing countries was that they should not be content to be "hewers of wood and drawers of water." To hasten the natural process of industrialization, developing-country governments encouraged the large-scale development of advanced manufacturing sectors. They did so by diverting private resources and public funds to subsidize manufacturing industries while discouraging traditional agricultural and resource extraction activities. Again, with the benefit of hindsight, it is clear that protection and targeting were misguided. Few infant industries ever became sufficiently productive to be weaned from public subsidies, and while some manufacturing industries did develop, the evidence (see chapter 3) indicates that developing countries could have grown *even faster* had they concentrated on their relative competitive advantage in resource-based activities.

In the 1980s and 1990s, targeting has again received a receptive audience in the United States and Europe, and again misperceptions of our economic performance are the driving force. Alarmist calls from policy makers have created the impression that industrial countries are at risk of losing their international economic power. Laura Tyson, President Clinton's chief economic adviser, warns that "we are teetering over the abyss of economic decline" and says that "the signs are everywhere: anemic productivity growth, falling real wages, a woefully inadequate educational system, and declining shares of world markets for many high technology products."[2] Alarmists point to industries like semiconductors, commercial aircraft, cellular telephones, and other large-scale, high-technology industries to make their argument that the United States is losing ground because of "unfair" foreign industrial and trade policies that subsidize foreign rivals and block imports. In short, proponents of targeting believe that the game of international competition is "winner take all" and that because the game had been rigged by foreign governments, we need to respond urgently and aggressively.

This line of reasoning has garnered support among policy makers, industry leaders, and the public. But while their claims have a superficial appeal, there are three fatal flaws in the arguments put forth by proponents of targeting. First, they use sweeping generalizations that often mask a country's true economic performance. It is true, for example, that in many high-technology sectors, such as electronics, the export market share of the United States declined during the 1970s and early 1980s. It is also true that declines in these sectors led to corresponding increases in Japanese market shares. In many other high-technology sectors, however, including chemicals, pharmaceuticals, computers, and aircraft, the United States expanded its market share and did so entirely at the expense of its Japanese rivals. Proponents of government intervention focus on the "losers" and often neglect the "winners" in international competition, perhaps in part because some of the most notable success stories have been in sectors with little direct U.S. government "assistance."

Second, interventionists believe that targeting works—that it can place domestic firms at a competitive advantage in world markets and disadvantage foreign rivals. Targeting proponents frequently cite examples of alleged Japanese targeting successes in industries such as semiconductors and color televisions. They typically neglect to mention, however, that only a handful of the more than sixty industries targeted by MITI (Japan's Ministry of International Trade and Industry) have ever achieved significant international success. Much more common are costly Japanese targeting *failures*—in industries ranging from steel to aluminum to aircraft to computers to biotechnology. Indeed, many of Japan's *true* success stories have been in industries such as home electronics and robotics, where the government has largely left private firms to compete freely against each other and internationally.

Finally, proponents regularly overstate the benefits and understate the costs of targeting. Benefits are overstated by ignoring the profits and employment that the same industry would have generated without targeting. In only a few cases does targeting actually *add* value. Costs are understated by ignoring the subsidy bill to taxpayers and the inflated price paid by the country's consumers. Costs are further understated by ignoring the effects of such policies on nontargeted industries. Targeting usually depresses other industries by diverting away capital and labor resources. Thus, even when rare targeting successes are achieved in one industry, the total return to the economy usually winds up being lower than without targeting.

It will be helpful to keep in mind these three flaws in a review of the claims made by targeting proponents and in a comparison of these claims against the actual record of targeting.

3
Targeting in Theory and in Practice

Proponents of targeting place their faith in five types of government policies. These are (1) subsidies to shift profits from a foreign to a domestic industry; (2) support for companies entering new markets; (3) assistance to promote exports; (4) subsidies to exploit "external economies," such as research where the benefits might spill over to those who have not paid the costs; and (5) policies to preserve domestic employment. A review of each of these targeting policies will show specifically why they have been costly failures.

Raising the Profits of Domestic Firms

Targeting proponents believe that direct government intervention can help domestic firms earn higher profits at the expense of their foreign competitors. One simple way to raise firms' profitability is to subsidize their operations. Popular targeting subsidies include defraying the costs of hiring employees, investing in research and development, and building additional plant capacity. In some cases, the government directly purchases the output of the firms at an inflated price, which boosts the firms' sales receipts and in turn their profits. In theory, these subsidies give firms a financial incentive to increase their production in pursuit of larger and larger payments from the government. Theory also says that research and plant capacity subsidies should cause domestic firms to invest more in research and production facilities, and this investment in turn should allow the firms to expand their future export operations as well. Theory predicts that foreign rivals might scale back their research and investment plans as well as their current production when they face a subsidized competitor. If they do, the profits of domestic firms can—in theory—grow even more as they gain a larger share of the world market.

For all these reasons, targeted subsidies could in *theory* raise domestic firms' profits. But in *practice*, firms' profits cannot be so easily manipulated by the government. A classic example is provided by Japan's targeting of its steel industry. Throughout the 1950s up through the early 1970s, Japanese steel firms were heavily subsidized with a combination of low tax rates and low-interest loans that were intended to subsidize the costs of raising capital for plant investments. The government subsidies led to a substantial expansion in steel production capacity, causing targeting proponents to claim the subsidies were successful. These proponents, however, confused higher industry *output* with higher industry *profits*. In fact, profit rates in Japan's steel industry were substantially below those for most other Japanese industries throughout the targeting period.

One of the main reasons that higher steel capacity and output did not translate into higher steel profits was that the government miscalculated how foreign producers would respond to Japanese subsidies. Rather than scaling back, as government officials predicted they would, foreign producers maintained their steel output—and sometimes actually increased output when they convinced their own governments to subsidize their operations in retaliation. The consequence of government-led capacity buildups was that world supply greatly exceeded world demand for steel. This imbalance drove down prices and profit margins. When the OPEC oil crisis further reduced steel demand in the 1970s, profits plunged even further.

By the start of the 1980s, Japanese steel firms were left with substantial idle capacity and were unable to cover their interest payments on past capital investments.[1] Japan's policies to subsidize its aluminum and nonferrous metal industries are two other examples of costly policy miscalculations that overexpanded production capacity, saturated world demand, and left firms unable to sell their output at a profitable price.

Lest one believe that only Japan has failed in its attempts to raise profits using targeted subsidies, Europe's steel industry tells much the same story. European governments have provided steel firms with low-interest loans and tax credits, protected their domestic markets from foreign competition with "voluntary" export quotas on Japan, and directly encouraged firms to collude on price and production levels in a concerted effort to raise industry profits. Despite all these government attempts to micromanage the steel industry, however, targeting again failed to raise profits, because it helped shield old, high-cost steel firms against competition from inside and outside Europe. It allowed firms that otherwise would have gone bankrupt to remain operating. Thus, the European steel policy turned out to be an expensive taxpayer bailout for shareholders and bondholders of bankrupt steel firms.[2]

Subsidizing New Firms to Enter the Market

A second type of targeting policy that is often touted by proponents is to subsidize firms' entry into the market. Developing countries have frequently relied on entry promotion theory to justify protecting nascent industries until they are capable of surviving on their own in the international market. Kozo Yamamura, a proponent of aggressive targeting, has argued that Japan's postwar success in entering world export markets was in large measure driven by protectionist, entry promotion policies. Yamamura claims that "as the firms expanded, the protected markets, which had served as hot houses for the fledgling industries, became export platforms easing the risk of aggressive expansion into export markets."[3]

My own research reveals little evidence that protecting industries eventually helps them boost exports.[4] Among a broad assortment of 200 U.S. manufacturing industries, I found that import protection had no perceptible effect on export performance. Nor did it help the industries where firms require extensive production experience at home to be internationally competitive. My research instead found that import barriers frequently made U.S. firms actually *less* competitive internationally, implying that the industries would have been more successful at exporting had the government not "assisted" them. Targeting failed to raise exports because it caused small, inefficient firms to enter the sheltered industry and reduced competitive pressures on existing firms to control their costs. By undermining the natural operation of the private marketplace, government targeting reduced competition. The brunt of this poor policy choice was borne by consumers who paid higher prices for protected goods.

There is a very simple reason why protected American industries usually continued to stagnate rather than grow through export expansion: trade protection treats only the symptoms of a declining industry—falling employment, idled plants, and a growing trade imbalance; it ignores the disease—inefficient, high-cost producers. Protection has only prolonged the inevitable departure of industry after industry, including steel, textiles, and shipbuilding. To keep these industries going, government would have to find the financial resources and political backbone to subsidize them forever. Fortunately, governments invariably lack the money, the will, or both. Competitive pressures eventually force declining industries to succumb to their inherent weaknesses and inefficiencies. Prolonging their inevitable death only prevents more efficient and growing sectors in the economy from acquiring all the resources that they need to prosper.

Evidence from other countries tells a very similar story. During the 1960s, Turkey and many other developing countries tried to nurture infant industries by shielding them from the pressures of foreign competition. Turkey attempted to raise productivity and encourage industrial development in industries such as petroleum refining, machinery, and chemicals. The results were unimpressive. Government-supported firms in these industries performed no better than firms that were forced to compete on equal terms with foreign rivals. And in some targeted industries such as petroleum refining, firms actually advanced *less* rapidly than those in other countries that were not coddled by subsidies. Even the targeted industries whose productivity grew most quickly, such as the rubber industry, grew at such a slow rate that it would have taken firms almost *twenty-five years* of sustained protection just to break even.[5] The same is true of targeting in Japan's and Korea's cotton textile industries. Government subsidies were needed for two, three, or even four decades to allow firms in these industries to break even. Thus, even if one ignores targeting's costs to taxpayers and consumers in the form of continuing subsidies and inflated prices, targeting still cannot be judged a success because it failed to allow infant industries to grow into profitable, self-sufficient ones.

The failure of targeting policies in these three countries to generate benefits over the long term directly undermines arguments that targeting provides important *dynamic* benefits. Proponents such as Laura Tyson stress that while targeting may not pass short-run cost-benefit tests, important dynamic (long-run) benefits from learning by doing can still tip the scales in favor of intervention. There are several reasons to doubt this claim. One comes from the evidence for Japan, South Korea, and Turkey that targeting remains a net drain on the economy for decades. A second reason is that politics always emphasizes immediate payoffs rather than long-term investment payoffs that might accrue long after the policy proponents are out of office. Thus, even if in theory targeting policies could be devised to yield long-term benefits, political incentives would work to undermine a long-term view.

Entry promotion policies have been equally unprofitable when they have been targeted at large, capital-intensive industries in developed countries. The United States has long claimed that European subsidies to the Airbus Consortium were instrumental in allowing Airbus to produce wide-bodied commercial aircraft in direct competition with its American rival, Boeing. Airbus borrows money at subsidized rates from the governments of France, Germany, the United Kingdom, and Spain. Government subsidies account for roughly 20 percent of Airbus's total budget. What have been the benefits and costs of this targeting exercise? On the benefits side, subsidies enabled Airbus to enter the market and gain roughly a one-third world market share. The costs are less visible, but they were many times larger. First, European taxpayers have footed the bill for Airbus subsidies, which total a staggering $11.5 billion. Second, and more important, the Airbus project diverted high-technology investment capital and skilled labor resources away from private projects that might well have earned an even higher rate of return. Thus, while Airbus in isolation looks like a break-even policy, the economy's total rate of return was actually reduced by having replaced private venture capitalists with government bureaucrats.

External Benefits

Industrial targeting proponents often argue that government intervention is justified when an industry generates "external benefits." An external benefit occurs when one firm invests in research and then rivals gain access to its technological discoveries without directly spending on research. Economic theory says that external benefits lead firms to "underinvest" in research from society's standpoint because the investing firm cannot fully appropriate the financial rewards from its innovation. In theory, government subsidies could reimburse researching firms for the external benefits that they create and could thereby help restore firms' research incentives. In practice, however, private markets can and do account for external benefits much more effectively than targeting proponents admit. Firms rely on technology licensing agreements and research joint ventures to share external benefits, and many American-Japanese high-technology partnerships have proved highly successful and profitable. By contrast, government policies to target research programs have usually been money-losing efforts that produced few external benefits to other firms or industries.

Targeting proponents often cite the semiconductor industry as an example where external benefits justify government intervention. Semiconductor research appears to have external benefits that spill over to other high-technology industries such as robotics and computers. To bolster its claims for protection against Japanese competitors, the U.S. Semiconductor Industry Association (SIA) claims that "the U.S. advantage in semiconductors has...enabled the U.S. to maintain a competitive lead in most other high technology fields."[6] The industry also claims that dynamic RAM memory chips are the "'bellwether for the industry'—the product that enables firms to reduce costs and enhance production in virtually all other semiconductor product lines."[7] SIA has been among the most vocal trade associations lobbying for direct government targeting. It believes that a temporary subsidy to establish market dominance in one generation of semiconductor chips could permanently shift advantage to American producers in future product generations.

Government policies to reap external benefits in the semiconductor industry, however, have been just as unfruitful as other targeting experiments. The U.S. government has tried to promote semiconductor research by relaxing antitrust laws to permit the Sematech research joint venture program.[8] In *theory*, cooperative joint ventures like Sematech could help firms as a group to exploit the external benefits from research and development. In addition, Sematech receives $100 million annually in direct government subsidies. In *practice*, Sematech has failed to improve semiconductor manufacturing technologies significantly, despite nearly a decade of government support. Sematech's bureaucratic management is antithetical to the flexibility and creativity essential to successful private research programs.

Moreover, American semiconductor firms have recently regained their international competitiveness by ignoring the misguided ideas underlying the government's Sematech experiment. Targeting proponents thought commodity-like memory chips were the key to industry success, and they focused government efforts on this commodity. They guessed wrong, however. American chip manufacturers have instead based their comeback on the growing market for the more complex logic chips. Targeting proponents thought that staying ahead in the business was possible only with continual, incremental improvements in chip manufacturing technology. Wrong again. Successful American chip manufacturers instead concentrated on their comparative advantage in developing innovative new chip designs. And targeting proponents thought that only large, vertically integrated firms or cartel-like consortiums could compete effectively against Japanese rivals. This was their third strike. The resurgence of the United States has been led by small, entrepreneurial upstarts, not by bureaucratic behemoths. Experience in the semiconductor industry demonstrates that government bureaucrats have little skill in directing research and development. No one understands the industry better than the firms that face the rewards and punishments of a private competitive market.

Government-led attempts to encourage high-technology

research in Japan have been equally misguided. MITI's targeting of the computer industry, contrary to many popular accounts, has left Japanese computer products lagging behind their competitors with little demand beyond their sheltered domestic market. Japan's Fifth Generation Computer Project, which began in 1983 as a well-funded ten-year effort to coordinate computer firms' research under government auspices, ultimately produced no fundamental technical advances or marketable products. Nor did it create important spillover benefits to other industries. Japanese government efforts to direct research for high-definition television (HDTV) led to the selection of an inferior and now obsolete technology, with the result that private American firms pursuing a more advanced digital standard are likely to dominate the early market for HDTV.

Britain's industrial policy experiments with the Concorde and advanced gas-cooled reactor provide additional evidence that targeting has failed to exploit external benefits to that country's advantage. To promote high-technology R&D and its potential spillover of knowledge to other industries, the British government sponsored development of a civil supersonic airplane, the Concorde, and a nuclear reactor, the advanced gas-cooled reactor, during the late 1950s. Approximately twenty years later, the Concorde and reactor programs finally entered commercial production and operation. A careful financial review of those industrial programs shows that in both cases the costs greatly outweighed the benefits.[9] It found that government investments in Concorde yielded a *negative* net return for taxpayers of about 6.5 percent per year. No private firm could have convinced shareholders or bondholders to lend on those terms. Concorde investments also generated few additional benefits to the economy, such as employment creation, increased exports, or technology spinoffs. The reactor program imposed costs on British consumers and taxpayers roughly equal to the Concorde project's losses. And both diverted investment capital and

17

skilled labor resources away from private, high-technology projects in Great Britain.

Preserving Jobs

Proponents of targeting also argue that aggressive trade and industrial policies are required to preserve "high skill, high wage employment opportunities" in manufacturing sectors.[10] While they sometimes acknowledge that efforts to protect domestic jobs with import barriers will lead consumers to pay higher prices, they believe that these costs are relatively small and are necessary for ensuring stable domestic employment. Proponents argue that the benefits of greater import competition and lower prices are little consolation if domestic workers lose their jobs to overseas competitors.

Policies to preserve employment and industries in decline try to reverse the natural evolution of competitive markets. As countries' technology and stage of economic development evolve, the products that they can produce most cheaply also change. It is unavoidable that some employees will be displaced and temporarily unemployed during transition periods, just as some suppliers of raw materials or capital will need to downsize temporarily. At the same time, however, new industries grow and develop new employment opportunities by attracting labor and capital from shrinking firms. These adjustments are best handled by private markets. Entrepreneurs know better than government bureaucrats how to make a smooth, efficient transition.

The costs of preserving employment through trade barriers are much, much larger than targeting proponents ever admit. The major disadvantage of government programs to preserve jobs in declining industries is that new industries are deprived of the employees that they need to grow. By artificially prolonging the life of less profitable, declining-wage industries and retarding growth in high-wage, profitable industries, government policies act like a brake on economic progress and the country's standard of living. It is possible to calculate just how costly industrial targeting has been when used to preserve jobs in declining industries. The costs include direct government outlays paid by taxpayers, the higher prices paid by consumers, and the forgone profits in new growth sectors. Those costs are always many times the wages earned by employees whose jobs are temporarily "saved" by targeting.

As an example, import barriers in the U.S. steel industry beginning in the early 1980s raised steelworkers' wages by $22,000 per job; yet each job saved in this industry cost U.S. consumers $750,000, or thirty-four times as much.[11] Other examples abound: the cost to U.S. consumers of saving jobs in the bolts, nuts, and screws industry was 100 times the benefit to that industry's workers. The cost of U.S. subsidies to maintain jobs in the U.S. dairy industry is $1,800 per cow, or greater than the per capita income of one-third of the world's population. At these rates, it would be cheaper simply to pay steelworkers, machine producers, and dairy farmers not to work. Because the total costs of preserving employment in declining industries are so large, this commonly heard rationale for targeting is actually the least persuasive.

Mimicking Japan and South Korea

Finally, targeting proponents usually hold Japan and South Korea up as models of trade and industrial policy "successes." A careful analysis, however, reveals a very different reality. Japan's unsuccessful experiment with targeting steel was described earlier. The government proved no better at micromanaging other heavy industries such as shipbuilding.[12] Starting in the 1950s, Japan raised its tariffs on British and West German ships to encourage the development of large, high-volume shipbuilding yards in Japan. As in

19

the steel industry, government investment subsidies led to an overbuilding of capacity. In the 1970s, when world demand fell and foreign competition rose, excess supply and low prices led to large financial losses for Japanese firms. The government was later forced to intervene again, this time to shrink the industry to one-quarter of its former size, effectively admitting that all its policies could not create a profitable shipbuilding industry. Large-scale failures also characterize Japanese targeting in agriculture, coal mining, oil refining, and petrochemicals.[13]

Failures by Japan's MITI have not been limited to smokestack industries. Government attempts to target high-technology "industries of the future" have been just as costly for its taxpayers and consumers. MITI has shown few tangible results from its persistent efforts to create profitable aircraft, aerospace, and biotechnology industries to encourage research and its potentially far-reaching benefits. Moreover, government bureaucrats have actually tried to block the private development of profitable high-technology industries because they did not mesh with MITI's grand design. One example of MITI obstruction occurred in the transistor industry. In 1953, Sony, then a small company, requested permission from the Japanese government to purchase transistor manufacturing rights from industry leader Western Electric in the United States. MITI's bureaucrats refused permission, expressing little confidence in Sony's future or in the value of transistor technology. Only Sony's perseverance enabled it to receive authorization after a long delay. Had MITI prevailed, Japan would never have developed one of its most successful exporting corporations. While Sony did eventually prevail, many other high-technology start-ups have been aborted by Japanese bureaucrats' shortsightedness and their inherent ignorance of markets.

Japanese targeting through direct public ownership of industries has also had disastrous results. Japan's national railway is known best for its high-speed bullet trains.

What is less well known is that until the government-owned agency was privatized in 1987, rail service in Japan was characterized by poor quality, frequent strikes, and operating losses averaging more than $20 million each day. The same is true for Japan's national airline. When Japan Air was finally privatized in 1987 and was forced to compete with foreign rivals for passengers, it found that years of government subsidies had left it incapable of competing successfully against private air carriers. Japan Air's share of traffic fell to one-sixth of its level before privatization, a drop that reflects the fact that years of subsidies allowed it to operate despite being one of the world's highest-cost air carriers.

Some U.S. policy advisers believe that informal industrial policies have played an important role in enhancing Japanese competitiveness.[14] These informal policies include export cartels, which promote firms' overseas sales, and administrative guidance, which steers firms' production and pricing decisions. Economic evidence, however, contradicts proponents' claims that MITI's informal policies have been productive. My own research showed that government-sponsored export cartels usually failed to affect the price, quality, or quantity of Japanese manufacturing industries' exports.[15] Japan's administrative guidance has also been largely ineffective.[16]

It is not surprising that Japan's informal targeting policies have failed to raise industrial productivity or competitiveness. Like many other countries, Japan has concentrated its targeting efforts in low-growth sectors, because political rather than economic considerations guide government targeting and low-growth sectors are the squeaky wheels that receive the grease of government support.

Perhaps the clearest assessment of Japanese targeting failures comes from Karl Zinsmeister, who has written:

> The list of industrial policy failures goes on and on. It is striking to note that many of Japan's feeblest industries are those that have been sub-

sidized by the government. Many of its strongest businesses—such as home electronics, cameras, robotics, precision equipment, pianos, bicycles, watches and calculators, numerically controlled machine tools, and ceramics—developed without help from MITI or other agencies. Japan achieved its economic miracle *not because of government planning but in spite of it.*[17]

Michael Porter of Harvard Business School gives an equally low grade to Japan's bureaucrats:

Government policy in a range of industries has had the effect of undermining competition and sheltering inefficient competitors, lowering the overall productivity of the Japanese economy....only a handful of the more than 60 industries [targeted by MITI and other agencies] have subsequently achieved significant international success.[18]

And David Henderson, a former senior staff economist on the President's Council of Economic Advisers, confirms that "the idea that central planning is responsible for Japan's success is a myth. MITI has made no contribution to many of Japan's biggest industrial successes."[19]

If targeted industrial policy has not provided the driving force behind Japanese growth, what has been responsible? The answer is entrepreneurial investment fueled by a high rate of private saving and encouraged by a low tax burden. Economist Hugh Patrick describes these growth forces:

Looking at Japanese industrial development as a whole in the postwar period...the predominant source of its success was the entrepreneurial vigor of private enterprise that invested a good deal and took a lot of risks. The main role of the government was to provide an accommodating and supportive environment for the market, rather than providing leadership or direction.[20]

Japanese private saving rates are roughly double those in the United States. Saving is strongly encouraged by Japan's low tax burden relative to other industrialized countries. Lower tax rates leave more money in the hands of business owners to save and invest. It is not a coincidence, therefore, that Japan's two decades of strongest postwar growth—1950 to 1970—were also its decades of lowest taxes. Japan's tax code also provides direct savings incentives by exempting large amounts of interest income from taxation and by not taxing capital gains from the sale of securities.[21]

Economist Katsuro Sakoh also attributes much of Japan's postwar growth to relatively limited micromanagement of its economy. Sakoh argues that "the government contribution is based not on how much it did for the economy, but on how much it restrained itself from doing."[22] At the same time, Japan pursued sensible and stable macroeconomic policies. Sakoh proceeds to argue that

> by maintaining a small and balanced budget, fairly low and stable interest rates, relatively low rates of taxation, stable prices, brief and mild recessions, [and] minimal defense and social welfare expenditures, the Japanese government helped provide an exceptionally favorable economic climate for private enterprise. Moreover, by maintaining the political stability necessary to promote private investment, the government contributed even further to increased economic growth.[23]

South Korea is second only to Japan in being cited as a targeting success. Korea has a long history of using trade and industrial policy to promote the export of targeted products. It actively undertakes many of the policies that are assumed to promote industrial competitiveness, such as tariff exemptions for imported inputs and capital equipment for export production, preferential tax treatment for both inputs to manufactured goods and export sales, reduced tax rates on export profits, subsidization of overseas market research, and formation of an export-import bank to provide export credit.

With all these supposedly export-promoting policies, Korean targeting has actually slowed economic growth. This conclusion may appear surprising at first—Korea has grown rapidly and achieved considerable success in exporting. But the relevant question to ask is what would have happened if the government had *not* intervened in its industrial development. A careful study by economists Don Gunasekera and Rod Tyers finds that Korea's economy would have grown 7 percent *faster* per year had Korea refrained from interventionist trade and industrial policies.[24] That is, targeting has not just been ineffective: it has actually been counterproductive.

Korean targeting favored dying (sunset) industries over emerging (sunrise) industries, discouraged firms from reducing their costs by lengthening their production runs, allowed small, inefficient producers to remain in many industries, and slowed gains in labor productivity in large-scale manufacturing industries. While a noninterventionist, open market policy would have increased imports into Korea, the Gunasekera and Tyers study calculates that Korean manufacturing firms would still have made productivity gains that could have expanded their total exports even while facing increased import competition. Industries such as textiles, lumber, and machinery would have experienced the greatest productivity increases and, accordingly, the greatest growth in exports. In other words, greater foreign competition would actually have helped Korean firms to grow by forcing them to become more efficient and productive. Safe behind high import barriers and receiving continual subsidies, Korean firms instead became content to grow more slowly.

The Korean government has had an equally bad record in targeting high-technology industries. A World Bank report found that subsidization of minicomputer development has created an industry heavily dependent on government purchases to cover its costs.[25] And like their Japanese counterparts, Korean bureaucrats initially opposed private firms' efforts to develop microcomputer and memory chip industries, which have since flourished into profitable industries. Once again, the private market proved to be a much wiser investor than government bureaucrats. As in other countries, consumers paid for the cost of inept bureaucratic management of the market. The World Bank report also found that targeting significantly raised prices paid by Korean consumers by limiting competition with imports and discouraging productivity gains by domestic firms. Policy activists conveniently omit that evidence when they claim targeting was a success.

After decades of failed experiments, Japan (and to a lesser degree Korea) has finally started to reverse its activist policies. The Japanese government has begun to weaken its rigid oversight of individual industries; to privatize its national railway, national airline, and government telephone monopoly; and to deregulate its oil refining and financial services industries. Japan's once tightly government-controlled retail and distribution sector has also been partially liberalized. And most recently, Japan has begun to lower its long-standing barriers to agricultural imports. Such signs that Japan is beginning to reject its interventionist past bode well for the future. It is ironic, however, that just as Japan is beginning to reject government micromanagement of business, some American and European policy makers are embracing that model.

4
Why Has Targeting Failed?

In industry after industry and country after country, government targeting and micromanaging of the economy have been only a burden to taxpayers and consumers. Targeting proponents, however, ignore these clear lessons from history, and their faith in intervention remains unshaken. They continue to recommend new policies to expand the reach of government to regulate firms.

To challenge the new activism successfully, we must understand not only targeting's history of failures but also why targeting can never work as claimed. Targeting is a futile endeavor because private markets can always outsmart government bureaucrats. Firms, investors, and consumers always find ways to circumvent the distorting effects of government intervention in a competitive world market. Foreign rivals always find ways to compete effectively for the profits that targeting tries to protect for domestic firms. Shareholders can always invest abroad, which severely limits a government's ability to control the economy. And consumers show remarkable flexibility in evading trade barriers and regulations. The power of political lobbying, the threat of retaliation, and bureaucrats' and economists' ignorance about industries are also very real problems that the theory of targeting fails to take into account. Each of these problems will continue to plague targeting policies. Understanding the true power of market forces to throw policy makers off their targets provides the best defense against future calls for government intervention.

Smaller Industry Profits

For targeting to raise a country's wealth, any profits that it generates have to exceed the costs of the policy. Industries such as commercial aircraft, steel, and semiconductors have frequently been targeted on the theory that profits would be high and sustainable long enough for targeting to raise national wealth. As the actual experience with targeting in these three industries showed, however, the costs far exceeded any profits.

In these and other industries, targeting resulted in a net loss of wealth in part because bureaucrats overestimated the size and duration of firms' profits. Few industries in fact earn the elevated profits necessary to outweigh the costs of targeting. Firms' monopoly power raises profits only on the order of 3 percent to 4 percent in U.S. manufacturing industries.[1] These low profits are unlikely to outweigh the cost to consumers who pay higher prices and the cost to taxpayers who pay for the subsidies. In addition, high profits are difficult to sustain in most industries. Except in a very small number of highly capital-intensive industries, competitors can successfully enter or remain in the market with a market share as small as 5 percent.[2] Thus, even if governments could raise profits in targeted industries, new domestic and foreign competitors for these firms would soon take a share of those elevated profits. A large number of competitors are not required to drive profits back down to a normal rate of return.

Targeting proponents frequently overstate the importance of barriers to entry, even in high-technology industries. And they underestimate just how strong competition is in industries, even when it takes several hundred million dollars to enter the market. But competition is vigorous, and entry is quite common, even in high start-up cost industries like semiconductors. Market shares and firms' rankings bounce continually from one generation of semiconductor chips to the next. While National Semiconductor was the world's leader in the 4K static RAM market, for

27

example, one product generation later the company had dropped out of the top five altogether. Its replacement was Hitachi—a company that had not even been in the static RAM market before. In EPROMs (electrical, programmable read-only memory chips), Hitachi bounced from number four to number one to number two to number five across successive product generations.[3] This continual leapfrogging has been repeated again and again in the semiconductor industry. Success is very short-lived in this industry because competition from even a few rivals is sufficient to displace today's top producer with tomorrow's leader.

Another problem with targeting high-profit industries is that often what looks like a high rate of profit is simply a return on an earlier, risky investment. Firms invest in research in the hope of receiving a competitive return to recoup their costs and compensate them for their risk. Some firms will meet this objective; others will not. The successful firms market their innovation; the unsuccessful ones never make it to the market, and therefore they remain invisible to economists. We may be tempted to conclude that the firms we can observe are earning elevated profits. An accurate measure of industry profits, however, should include the losses of the unsuccessful firms that never reached the market. Without knowing which industries are truly earning an elevated profit, therefore, policy makers are shooting in the dark. Private investors are much better informed than government bureaucrats about which industries offer the best profit opportunities. They have to be, because unlike bureaucrats, their own money is at stake—not taxpayers'.

Foreign Investments Undermine Targeting

The arguments of targeting proponents rely heavily on the assumption that government policy can clearly discriminate between domestic and foreign firms. Profit-shifting policies, for example, are intended to redistribute profits away from foreign rivals and toward domestic producers and consumers. Targeting supporters, however, fail to recognize that in the world of business, national boundaries are rapidly becoming extinct. Many U.S. corporations, for example, produce overseas and import their products to the United States. In fact, one-third of total U.S. merchandise imports are manufactured by foreign-based affiliates of American corporations. Moreover, one-fifth of U.S. merchandise exports are produced by foreign-owned companies producing in the United States.[4] In the current interdependent world, IBM has become Japan's largest exporter of computers, and Sony is the largest exporter of televisions from the United States.

Economic integration and foreign direct investment severely complicate a government's efforts to discriminate between domestic and foreign firms when choosing which industries to target. David Angel raises the central question when he asks, "Is government support to be directed toward U.S.-owned firms, or toward all firms (domestic or foreign) operating within the United States? In the face of increasing internationalization of production, it is far from clear whether support for U.S.-owned firms will translate into the greatest number of high income jobs for U.S. workers."[5] And government policies that ignore the move toward international integration lead to highly perverse situations, such as a recent case in which the U.S. government offered to protect a Japanese firm assembling typewriters in the United States against competition by an American firm importing typewriters into the United States from its plant in Singapore.

Any proposal for targeting that does not take international shareholding and investment into account will overestimate the policy's potential benefits. Briefly, when an American-based firm is partially foreign owned, any profits that targeting generates must be shared with foreign shareholders. And if foreign-based firms likewise have some American shareholders, these investors will suffer a capital loss if targeting succeeds in shifting profits away from the foreign firms and toward their U.S. rivals. In this way, U.S. residents receive only a portion of the potential benefits and also bear some of the costs of targeting. The actual return to shareholders from targeting is therefore much smaller than the return suggested by simple theories.

My recent research has shown how even modest international shareholding and investment dramatically reduce a country's gains from targeted subsidies.[6] In 1987, for example, foreign direct and portfolio ownership in U.S. manufacturing averaged 14.0 percent while the corresponding share of U.S. ownership abroad was approximately 3.4 percent. Despite the fact that these shares seem small, they have a big influence on who gains and who loses from targeting. When one takes into account this magnitude of cross-ownership between American and foreign firms, the potential gains from a U.S. subsidy to exports fall by one-half. In other words, targeting proponents have claimed that benefits are *twice* what might reasonably be expected.

But this is not the end of the story. The benefits of targeting fall by another one-quarter when one takes account of international tax rules. In general, firms' profits are taxed on the basis of where income is earned rather than where it is repatriated. Thus, even if targeted firms do earn higher profits (a rarity, as we have seen earlier), much of those profits would go to foreign governments in the form of taxes. In American industries such as petroleum, chemicals, and pharmaceuticals, firms earn much of their revenues overseas. In these industries, I found that international cross-ownership and tax laws completely eliminate any potential gain from targeted export subsidies. In fact, in some of these cases, strategic trade policy would imply that the government should *tax* rather than subsidize domestic firms' exports. Thus, not only have targeting proponents greatly overstated the gains from export subsidies, but in some industries they have recommended exactly the wrong policy according to their own theories.

Protection and Domestic Production

In theory, targeting could increase firms' profits if it caused domestic firms to raise their output and foreign competitors to respond by contracting production. When foreign rivals respond by cutting back their output, prices rise and the targeted firms enjoy both higher output and a higher price. The more that the domestic expansion occurs at the expense of sales by foreign rivals, the greater could be the increase in domestic firms' profits from the targeting policy.

In practice, however, protection has typically been ineffective at raising production in targeted industries or even reversing contractions in depressed sectors.[7] More efficient foreign suppliers usually find legitimate ways to thwart policy makers' attempts to favor domestic producers at their expense. They have shown great aptitude at outsmarting even the best laid plans of American protectionists. Japanese firms exporting to the United States, for example, have frequently lowered their profit margin rather than yield market share to domestic suppliers targeted for special protection.[8] In many textile and footwear industries, foreign producers have responded to limits on their exports by raising the quality of their products; domestic producers then had to compete with them by raising product quality and thus costs.[9]

Another common response by foreign firms is to export their product in a more or less processed form to circumvent targeting. Two recent examples illustrate how this works. When the United States recently raised its tariff on assembled truck imports, it left the tariff on unassembled vehicles unchanged. To evade the higher tariff on assembled imports, Japanese exporters switched from exporting assembled to exporting unassembled trucks to the United States, where they simply completed the final assembly stages. As a result, American truck producers were no better off than before. A second example occurred in the semiconductor and computer circuit board industries. To avoid tightened U.S. restrictions on the importation of uninstalled semiconductor chips, Japanese firms exported assembled circuit boards with the chips already installed, again undercutting the anticipated level of protection for American chip producers. These and other offsetting supply responses explain why targeting usually fails to raise domestic production and, in turn, profits.

Protection and Costs

While targeting does not usually raise production, it does usually raise costs by "protecting" firms from the beneficial effects of foreign competition. Under targeting, costs rise for either of two reasons. First, targeting can lead relatively less efficient producers to enter the industry in anticipation of receiving a subsidy. Entry by firms that otherwise would have been unprofitable will lower the industry's average profitability. Historical experience shows that competition is the best medicine for sickly industries: when they are subjected to more, not less, international competition, costs fall and inefficient firms leave the industry. Large across-the-board reductions in Canadian manufacturing tariffs during the 1970s, for example, led small, relatively higher-cost producers to leave the industry. This allowed the remaining, more efficient firms to expand by taking further advantage of efficiencies resulting from large-scale production.[10] Lowering trade protection also raised productivity in Australian, South Korean, and Turkish manufacturing industries. It follows from these experiences that protectionism—which shields targeted domestic firms from international competition—will raise costs and reduce efficiency.

A second reason that firms' costs increase is that targeting may inadvertently raise the price of scarce inputs to production. An export subsidy can bid up demand for a scarce input and therefore raise its price. The higher input price increases firms' costs, and this reduces their profits, the net of revenues minus costs. This problem has arisen in industries that use unionized labor. If targeting increases the industry's demand for labor, the union will usually succeed in bidding the wage rate up to capture a portion of the industry's higher anticipated profits. When the union also supplies labor to other industries, those industries will also experience a fall in profits because their wage costs have risen. In both targeted and nontargeted sectors, then, targeting can turn out to be an expensive policy whose only winner is unionized labor.

Economists and Bureaucrats Are Not Omniscient

Perhaps if governments had perfect foresight and understood completely how private markets operate, targeting could work. Targeting proponents envisage a complex web of government monitoring and oversight of industries that will ultimately force markets to carry out their wishes. But private firms and investors are smarter than both economists and bureaucrats. In addition, governments cannot predict with accuracy how foreign competitors or governments will respond to targeting policies. Japan's targeting of its steel industry, for example, was premised on the government's expectation that foreign firms would scale back production. When American and European firms instead responded by holding their production stable, a glut on world steel markets depressed Japanese prices and profits. Similar miscalculations undermined Japanese targeting in its aluminum and nonferrous metals industries.

The semiconductor industry offers another illustration of how governments can misjudge market responses. Europe and Japan adopted quite similar trade and industrial policies to nurture a domestic semiconductor industry. In both places, tariffs were high, nontariff barriers further helped to block imports, and research was directly subsidized. An important difference lay in the governments' choices of which type of semiconductors to promote. Japan encouraged its firms to produce commodity-like memory chips such as DRAMs,[11] to allow them to hone their manufacturing skills on large production runs. Europe, in contrast, encouraged its firms to produce more specialized, proprietary chips whose relatively short production runs did not allow firms to develop the state-of-the-art manufacturing skills that eventually came to drive industry fortunes. Could the "correct" choice have been predicted at the outset? Probably not. Was government better situated to make an informed choice between chip types? Again, probably not. In a highly uncertain environment, Europe and Japan gambled on different strategies, and only one was a winner.

The ignorance of economists and bureaucrats is a crucial weakness. Even relatively small changes in economic conditions can reduce or even reverse the effects of policies. Since economists cannot reliably predict such effects, the safest course is to leave undisturbed the smooth functioning of private markets.

Targeting Provokes Trade Partners

Targeting invariably invites retaliation. Virtually all the targeting cases reviewed earlier led to some form of retaliation: examples include American commercial aircraft subsidies in retaliation against Airbus subsidies, U.S. price floors on Japanese semiconductor imports in retaliation against alleged dumping, and American retaliation against steel targeting by Japan and other Asian producers. The United States, Japan, and the European Community are all politically and philosophically predisposed to retaliate against any foreign targeting threats. The situation is aggravated because each of these governments is anxious to stake claims in the same "strategic," high-technology industries. In these sectors, trading partners are unlikely to remain passive if one country adopts policies to strengthen the comparative advantage of its firms. But experience has clearly shown that retaliation usually leaves the trading partners worse off than before. Therefore, government agreements not to wield industrial and trade policies as weapons can be to the mutual benefit of all countries.

What Drives Protection?

The greatest weakness of targeting proponents is their blindness to the reality that political forces ultimately drive trade policy. Firms lobby government representatives for targeting, contribute to candidates that support their positions, and petition administrative and regulatory bodies for favorable policy rulings. Their efforts are not in vain. In practice, protection is awarded more frequently in response to an intense lobbying effort instead of on the merits of the case. The 1986 Semiconductor Trade Agreement negotiated between Japan and the United States, which effectively cartelized the industry at the expense of consumers, illustrates this fact. Dedicated lobbying by this small industry, combined with effective threats of continued antidumping suits against Japanese exporters, led the government to protect American semiconductor firms. As chapter 7 will explain, most of the gain went to Japanese producers while American consumers—whose voices were lost in the political debate—paid higher prices and faced supply shortages. Politics also drives targeting in other countries, including Japan. Analysis by Katsuro Sakoh concluded that "the overwhelming bulk of government financial support in Japan has been distributed to politically powerful groups."[12]

Politics not only creates egregious policies in the first place but also works to ossify them. The policies become politically untouchable, never to be disturbed for fear of angering vested industry interests. Import quotas, tariffs, and industrial subsidies continue long after any original policy motivation has disappeared. The longer these policies remain, the longer their inefficiencies drain wealth from consumers, taxpayers, and other sectors of the economy whose growth is stunted. A critic notes:

> Governments...confuse job creation with wealth creation. It is hard for them to close down firms that are not doing well. Such money losing tendencies are reinforced by congressional representatives, mayors and local constituencies that lobby to keep losers open, hoping for a better future.[13]

Charles Schultze, chairman of the Council of Economic Advisers under President Carter, echoes this view when he labels government the "universal protector of inefficiency." Schultze argues that "the formal and informal institutions of the political system are designed to hinder government from making hard choices among specific individuals, rewarding some and penalizing others."[14] While the private market makes these hard choices efficiently, governments follow the path of least political resistance. Thus, Schultze notes that "for every twenty new entrants into the high-tech race, nineteen will probably perish and only one will succeed. But the federal government's portfolio would likely carry all twenty forever."[15]

5

Semiconductors—
No Exception to the Rule

Despite the preponderance of examples in which governments misjudged the wisdom of the private market, a small and influential cadre of academics and policy makers continues to search for "winning industries" to favor with government largesse. The semiconductor industry has emerged as a sentimental favorite for these policy activists. Thus, the president's economic adviser, Laura Tyson, maintains that "although government regulation has been widely discredited in many sectors, there is no presumption that the visible hand of policy in semiconductors will lead to lower economic welfare than the invisible hand of the market."[1] Tyson forgets, however, that the visible hand usually winds up deep inside taxpayers' pockets.

Policy activists favor targeting semiconductors to level the international playing field, safeguard national defense, take advantage of external benefits, preserve domestic jobs, and reap other "strategic" benefits. An analysis of each of these arguments in turn will show why they are no more persuasive when applied to the semiconductor industry than to other industries. The fundamental reason why targeting fails in high-technology industries, according to Intel's CEO Andrew Grove, is that they resist central guidance. According to Grove, industries such as computers and semiconductors represent "industrial democracies" that grow from the bottom up by private initiative, not from the top down by government directive.[2]

The track record of targeting in semiconductors is littered with failed attempts to outsmart the market. Three policy case studies summarize well the costs and failures of such targeting. The first concerns charges by U.S. firms that their Japanese competitors were "dumping" memory chips at distress prices during the mid-1980s. While these charges had little economic justification, the industry successfully persuaded the Department of Commerce to impose higher tariffs on Japanese semiconductor imports. These tariffs were supposed to help U.S. chip producers, but their primary effect was to hurt U.S. consumers by forcing them to pay significantly higher prices for computer chips. This policy failure is chronicled in chapter 6. The dumping dispute prompted a second industry intervention, which was the creation of a government-enforced cartel agreement between U.S. and Japanese producers. The agreement, signed in 1986 and renewed in 1991, raised chip prices to new heights and again hurt U.S. consumers, this time providing windfall profits to Japanese producers. As chapter 7 explains, Japan used these profits to fund research toward the next generation of computer chips, leaving U.S. firms even further behind. The final industrial policy experiment that is reviewed, in chapter 8, is the Sematech research consortium. Sematech is a government-backed project that sought to propel chip manufacturers into the next generation of technologies but wound up being only a costly bailout of failing U.S. equipment suppliers.

Leveling the Playing Field

The most commonly offered justification for targeting semiconductors is probably the need to "level the playing field." Targeting proponents credit the success of Japan's semiconductor industry to the Japanese government's targeting policies.[3] Viewing the Japanese experience as the prototype for strategic intervention, proponents argue that the United States has much to learn from Japanese policy "successes." David Angel summarizes this view when he writes,

> Through a combination of investment incentives, coordination of R&D, and market closure, the Japanese government helped to secure the rise of the Japanese semiconductor industry to a position of market leadership, thereby undermining the profitability of, and employment in, the U.S. semiconductor industry. By this account, the United States should learn from the Japanese experience and implement a national technology and trade initiative of its own, one designed to ensure the competitiveness of U.S. firms in global markets.[4]

Calls to level the playing field and to replicate Japanese targeting seem sensible and appealing—at first glance. But a careful review of market conditions undermines this appeal.

First, since the industry's inception, the U.S. government has assisted semiconductor producers just as the Japanese government has. Both countries pursued infant industry policies in which the government nurtured fledgling firms through a combination of direct subsidies and a secure home market sheltered from foreign competition. In the United States, the subsidies came largely through Department of Defense research projects, and the agency also acted as the industry's largest purchaser during its infancy. With a guaranteed demand for their products and significant defraying of the risks of investing in uncertain research projects, U.S. semiconductor firms overwhelmingly dominated the industry through the late 1970s.[5] During formative stages in its semiconductor industry in the late 1970s, Japan also sponsored research (frequently through government-led joint ventures) and safeguarded the domestic market through a combination of formal and informal barriers. Like their American counterparts, Japanese semiconductor firms welcomed government favors but vigorously resisted attempts by bureaucrats to micromanage their business decisions or to attach strings to government aid. The view that Japanese industry and government work hand in hand is largely a fiction, especially in the semiconductor industry.

Second, the notion that U.S. firms face unfair competition is largely a myth. Japan's government does continue to aid its semiconductor industry, but the U.S. government is equally or even more active in granting support in many areas. During the second half of the 1980s, for example, U.S. government support for semiconductor research and development outstripped Japanese government support by a ratio of ten to one.[6] The claims of U.S. firms that they are fighting an unfair match are not supported by market share data, either. The share of the Japanese semiconductor market held by U.S. firms exceeded Japan's share of the American market up until the mid-1980s, and the two shares were roughly comparable for a few more years afterward.[7] Broadly speaking, U.S. producers overwhelmingly dominated their domestic market, while Japanese producers likewise dominated their domestic market. The two countries split the European and other Asian markets, with U.S. firms holding a slightly larger share in Europe because of their long-standing direct investments in production facilities in Europe. This is hardly the tilted playing field claimed by targeting proponents.

Finally, blaming the lackluster track record of American semiconductor firms selling in Japan on that country's "unfair" trade and industrial policies is naïve. A careful analysis of Japan's success in the world market reveals that it stems largely from the ability of private firms to back the right technologies. As Brink Lindsey argues, "The great breakthroughs in microelectronics have been driven by entrepreneurial innovation, not industrial policy."[8] An example is given by the competition between CMOS and

NMOS technologies for chip production. Japanese firms pioneered CMOS technology, which is used in production of low-cost logic devices for products such as watches and calculators. American firms, in contrast, backed NMOS technology, which they used in production of computer memory chips. In the early 1980s, innovations in lithographic equipment for chip manufacturing lowered the cost of using CMOS techniques significantly below the cost for NMOS, which previously had been the lower-cost technology. As Dieter Ernst and David O'Connor relate, "All of a sudden, the long acquaintance of the Japanese with CMOS technology turned out to be an important competitive advantage. For the now predominant process technology, Japanese firms were in a better position than their American counterparts to improve yields and to deliver new memory generations."[9] Thus, Japan's success was driven primarily by the combination of informed private decisions and fortuitous circumstances—contrary to the popular belief that MITI's guidance led Japanese firms to make successful research and production choices.

National Defense

Another frequently raised claim is that the semiconductor industry must be protected to safeguard national defense. No one would argue that semiconductors are not an important component of U.S. weapons and security systems, because they form the basis for most microelectronic gadgetry. Seizing these facts, many targeting proponents argue that military preparedness demands that the government protect the U.S. semiconductor industry. They want the public to believe that the *only* way to guarantee a secure supply of chips for defense applications is to protect every firm in the U.S. semiconductor industry. In reality, the national defense argument for semiconductor targeting obscures the real facts and is based on highly improbable assumptions.

An important fact that targeting proponents overlook is that the U.S. military's demand for semiconductors represents less than one-tenth of 1 percent of worldwide demand.[10] Put differently, over 99.9 percent of total world chip supplies would have to be monopolized by other users to create a shortage for the defense industry. Even under this highly unlikely scenario, the existing production base in the United States has more than sufficient capacity to meet the demands of the military if necessary.

It is curious why targeting proponents believe that the entire semiconductor industry requires protection for national security reasons when, in fact, only a handful of specialty companies produce semiconductor chips used for defense applications. Defense-purpose chips must be built to withstand temperature extremes and radiation levels, which requires that they be specially designed and manufactured at considerable additional cost. Most U.S. firms focus their production instead on the commercial market, which does not demand these specifications. Given the facts, protecting the entire commercial semiconductor industry is a very roundabout—and very costly—"solution" to the problem of ensuring defense supplies.

A realistic solution to concerns about national security need not involve the costs and inefficiencies associated with protecting an entire industry. A cheaper and more pragmatic alternative is for the military to produce its own chips in-house or, almost equivalently, write long-term procurement contracts with the few firms that currently focus on the defense market. This solution would much more closely meet the goal of guaranteeing a secure supply of the type of chips that defense contractors need. Under this policy, the Department of Defense would act much like any other (private) chip buyer would. Like other buyers, the department would rely on the private market to make informed research and production decisions. The targeting policy instead would require the department to take on the impossible role of trying to second-guess and manage an entire industry.

Taking Advantage of External Benefits

Targeting proponents believe that semiconductor firms need the government to encourage their research and to help prevent foreign companies from profiting from U.S. discoveries. These notions are grounded in the basic premise that the government knows better than private companies how to conduct their business.

According to targeting proponents, the government should encourage semiconductor research because the benefits flow far beyond just the firms that carry out the research. Those benefits are frequently referred to as research "spillovers." Spillovers may come from competitors that reverse-engineer new chip designs, rivals that hire away other firms' engineers to learn about their research projects, and computer manufacturers that gain insights for their own design problems from observing chip manufacturers' plans. Many others in the economy can benefit from one firm's research spending, but these benefits do not usually enter into the researching firm's decision about how much to invest in R&D. Because of this, firms could underinvest in research from society's viewpoint. Targeting proponents argue that government subsidies will be needed to encourage private firms to increase their research investment to reflect the full benefits that accrue to society.

The validity of this argument for targeting rests precariously on a series of assumptions, none of which fits the semiconductor industry very well. First, the argument assumes that firms do not know how to capture the financial return from their research spending. In fact, however, firms actively use private markets for this purpose, by forming research joint ventures, negotiating technology licensing contracts, and arranging to share production facilities. The semiconductor industry has hundreds of these private business arrangements, both among U.S. firms and between U.S. and Japanese firms. The firms have developed effective business arrangements to capture the return to

43

their research. In light of this, the burden of proof lies with proponents of targeting to explain why semiconductor firms need government assistance.

Targeting proponents also prematurely jump to the conclusion that firms spend "too little" on research for the good of society. Seeking to justify government research subsidies to semiconductor firms, proponents fail to see the complete picture presented by an impartial economic analysis. Economists regard research as a race among firms that compete aggressively to develop innovations and beat each other to the marketplace. The research departments of semiconductor firms strive to be the first in the industry to introduce each new chip design. The winner begins the race to the manufacturing stage, where it will accumulate the knowledge and experience to improve product quality and lower production costs. The race naturally involves some duplication of research effort by firms competing to invent new chip designs. From society's standpoint, on the one hand, firms will invest too much in R&D because duplicated research wastes engineering talent and funds that could have been directed to other research projects. On the other hand, the fact that the benefits to research can spill over tends to encourage too little research. What is the *net* effect? Economic theory tells us that both of these forces are at work—it cannot tell us for certain which one will dominate. By choosing to mention only one part of the picture, targeting proponents misleadingly cite "failures" of the invisible hand as a justification for government research subsidies.

In their drive for government support, targeting proponents do not admit that foreign companies benefit from government research subsidies given to U.S. firms—but they do. In the semiconductor industry, chip designs and know-how about manufacturing process technologies spill quickly across borders and automatically allow foreign producers to benefit from increased U.S. research activity. A careful study of manufacturing technology diffusion in the semiconductor industry reveals that improvements spill just as quickly from American to Japanese firms as they do within the United States.[11] Therefore, a policy favoring research by U.S. firms will equally benefit Japanese competitors. Targeting proponents overlook the fact that because semiconductor manufacturing has become increasingly globalized, it is therefore harder for governments to help domestic firms and not their overseas competitors.

Preserving Jobs

In policy circles, targeting is seen as an acceptable policy for preserving jobs threatened by international competition. Targeting has been used to preserve jobs in the declining steel, textile, and automobile industries, in the belief that massive job dislocation and downward wage spirals would be the inevitable result of unchecked import competition. Although semiconductors are a sunrise rather than a sunset industry, policy makers see targeting as helping to retain high-skilled, high-paying semiconductor jobs. The same fallacies that plague arguments for preserving employment in other industries, however, also undermine the rationale for targeting semiconductor jobs. Targeting is costly and, ultimately, powerless at thwarting natural labor market forces.

Targeting the semiconductor industry has cost millions of dollars in direct research and defense procurement subsidies, plus the billions of dollars in artificially higher prices paid by chip consumers. The entire U.S. semiconductor industry, however, employs only 175,000 people.[12] Even assuming that every one of these jobs is at risk of disappearing—a highly questionable assumption—the cost of saving each job is in the hundreds of thousands of dollars. While purposely downplaying this astronomical cost, targeting proponents also overlook the strong possibility that their policies merely save one job at the expense of another. Employment may fall in industries that must purchase higher-priced inputs because of trade protection. Economist Arthur Denzau has calculated that for each job "saved" in the semiconductor industry by the 1986 U.S.-Japan trade agreement, for example, another was lost in computer manufacturing as higher chip prices drove down computer demand.[13]

Moreover, even if domestic employment eroded, many displaced semiconductor workers have ready employment alternatives. The majority of the industry's employees—some 89,000 employees—work in executive, professional, and clerical positions. Many semiconductor production-line workers are also technically skilled and relatively mobile. Both groups of employees would suffer few of the market frictions and job-hunting difficulties that unskilled workers face when they are displaced. Only a small proportion of the industry's work force might suffer from long-term difficulties if they were forced to change employers. Direct job retraining and relocation assistance is a much more practical and affordable alternative compared with providing massive subsidies and protectionist umbrellas that distort an entire industry for the sake of relatively few jobs.

Other "Strategic" Considerations

When other arguments fail to persuade, semiconductor targeting advocates resort to appeals to the industry's "strategic" nature. International trade lawyer Brink Lindsey notes that "strategic industries are a dime a dozen. Every decent lobbyist can come up with several plausible sounding reasons why the industry he represents is a linchpin of American economic strength and therefore must be preserved at all costs."[14] Ultimately, however, very few industries actually meet the criteria of being truly strategic. An industry is deemed strategic by economists if it has the long-term potential to sustain unusually high profits, perhaps because it is difficult for other firms to enter the market and drive down prices. Earlier, it was explained how in theory subsidizing or protecting domestic firms' operations could allow them to gain larger market share and a larger share of the industry's profits. It was also explained how in practice firms' profits cannot so easily be manipulated by governments. Governments may miscalculate how foreign competitors will respond to their intervention, or they may just encourage subsidized firms to grow lazy and see their higher potential profits eroded away by escalating costs. Very few industries are able to avoid these practical pitfalls and qualify as truly strategic.

The semiconductor industry especially fails the definition of a strategic industry, because firms simply do not earn unusually high rates of profit over long periods of time. Historically, semiconductor producers have earned a rate of return that is close to the average for all manufacturing industries over the business cycle. The high profits that individual firms have earned from time to time have been transitory, usually lasting only as long as the current product generation.[15] This is not surprising. Firms regularly leapfrog over one another to become the new market leader each time that chip technologies change. All it takes is a handful of rivals to keep competition dynamic and vigorous. Under these highly competitive conditions, there is little chance that firms will be able to earn and sustain the kind of profits envisaged by targeting proponents. When there are not large profits to redistribute, the rationale for government intervention disappears.

6
Managing Semiconductor Trade

S ince the industry's birth, semiconductor trade has
been manipulated on both sides of the Pacific as activist governments sought to boost their firms' share
of industry sales and profits. Starting in the mid-1980s, the
United States moved beyond just manipulating trade and
began directly regulating the price and quantity of semiconductor imports and exports. The U.S. semiconductor
industry aggressively lobbied for direct government management of its trade with Japan, fearing that without intervention the industry would be unable to penetrate Japanese
markets and would be driven from its own market by "predatory" Japanese business practices. The industry skillfully
used U.S. trade laws to its own narrow advantage in an effort to restrict Japanese semiconductor imports, while at
the same time demanding that Japan accept more U.S.
semiconductor exports.

On the export side, the U.S. industry asserted that its
firms did not face a level playing field abroad. The industry claimed that a wide array of import barriers denied
them "fair and equitable opportunities" for selling in the
Japanese market. The use of the term *opportunities* was critical. The U.S. industry argued that if they were only given a
fair opportunity to compete against Japanese rivals, American exports would rise dramatically. We have already seen
how, in reality, the United States and Japan *both* adopted

protectionist policies that denied foreign rivals export opportunities. Despite the fact that both countries were at-
tempting to tilt the playing field to their firms' advantage,
the U.S. industry convinced policy makers to threaten Japan with sanctions by the General Agreement on Tariffs
and Trade (GATT) unless it abandoned its protectionist
policies. During the 1970s, U.S. threats succeeded at forcing Japan to increase its imports of U.S. computers and
computer components, including semiconductors. By the
end of the decade, Japan had essentially eliminated all formal trade barriers in its semiconductor industry.

Improving export opportunities, however, did not lead
to an immediate rise in U.S. semiconductor exports to Japan. Instead, over the next several years the U.S. share of
the Japanese market remained at its traditional 10 percent
level. Faced with its failure to compete successfully despite
government assistance, the U.S. industry shifted away from
demanding "equal opportunities" and toward demanding
"equal outcomes." To implement this new demand, the
industry filed a petition under section 301 of the Trade
Act of 1974 demanding that Japan take immediate steps
to increase the market share of U.S. firms. The industry
failed to explain why it warranted government intervention when, up until the mid-1980s, the United States actually occupied a *larger* share of the Japanese market than
Japanese firms occupied in the United States. The industry also failed to provide compelling and persuasive evidence that Japanese import barriers were to blame for its
lackluster export performance. Actually, the relatively small
Japanese market share of U.S. firms appears largely explain-
able by quality and marketing deficiencies. American chips
tended to be more susceptible to defects and performance
problems, and U.S. firms often refrained from investing
in direct marketing facilities in Japan. Despite all the economic evidence opposing their demand for equal outcomes, however, U.S. firms convinced Washington to
pressure Japan into guaranteeing them a fixed share of

the Japanese semiconductor market. These demands ultimately led the two governments to establish a cartel agreement regulating semiconductor exports, as I explain in detail in chapter 7.

On the import side, U.S. firms claimed that they were the victims of "predatory pricing" by Japanese firms selling in the American market. In June 1985, Micron Technologies formally filed an antidumping legal complaint against seven Japanese competitors, alleging that they were selling 64K DRAMs at below-cost prices or dumping in the U.S. market. Micron argued that its Japanese competitors would eventually drive it out of business and then raise prices and reap monopoly profits. In August, the International Trade Commission (ITC) issued a preliminary ruling that concluded that Japanese semiconductor imports had injured U.S. producers by depressing their sales and profits.

The next month, three other U.S. firms (Advanced Micro Devices, Intel, and National Semiconductor) filed suit charging that Japanese firms were also dumping EPROMs in the U.S. market. In November, the ITC gave its blessing to this second dumping complaint. In the months that followed, the Department of Commerce ruled in favor of the U.S. industry and levied preliminary fines against Japanese exporters based on the department's estimate of the degree of below-cost pricing. Finally, in an unprecedented action, the Department of Commerce initiated its own dumping complaint against Japanese firms selling 256K and 1 megabyte DRAMs. As chapter 7 will explain, this succession of dumping complaints provided the second driving force behind the efforts of the two governments to form an international semiconductor cartel.

Were the industry's dumping charges justified, or did they instead simply represent an attempt by a troubled industry to gain protection from more efficient foreign competitors? While the U.S. semiconductor industry is popularly portrayed as the victim of Japanese predatory pricing, the industry's antidumping complaints were actually a calculated strategy designed to place Japanese rivals at a disadvantage in the U.S. market. In fact, U.S. companies invoked antidumping laws to penalize foreign firms for the very same practices that they themselves were following. The U.S. industry charged Japanese firms with selling at prices that apparently prevented them from recouping their costs of production. Calculating production costs, however, is a complex task in the semiconductor industry. A firm's average cost of production depends crucially on the "yield" that it achieves during the manufacturing process. The yield is defined by the percentage of chips that are free from defect and thus that can be sold on the market. In semiconductor production, yields rise quickly over the product cycle as firms gain production experience and hone their manufacturing skills. Economists often refer to this phenomenon as "learning by doing."[1] As a firm's yield rises, its average cost of producing a salable chip falls.

In the semiconductor industry, therefore, firms make their production decisions knowing that the more they produce today, the more experience they will gain and the higher their future yield will be. Pricing decisions will reflect these dynamics of learning by doing. Thus, a long-standing practice among American semiconductor firms—which predates Japan's entry into the industry—is to engage in "forward pricing." Forward pricing means that the firm sets a price that yields a profit when total revenues and costs are summed up over the complete product cycle. In early years of the product cycle, however, the firm may take short-term losses because its chip yield is low. When firms forward price, they will appear to be dumping—that is, their costs may exceed their revenues. Indeed, according to the strict letter of U.S. law, these firms will be dumping. But their pricing represents sensible, competitive behavior and is a widespread practice—not necessarily a predatory strategy designed to drive rivals out of business.

7
The Government
Semiconductor Cartel

While the market access and antidumping complaints of U.S. semiconductor firms had little economic support, the industry skillfully courted both public opinion and policy makers' attention. The Semiconductor Industry Association hired a public relations firm, organized a support group within Congress, and actively lobbied the administration. Under industry pressure, in 1986 the U.S. trade representative (USTR) and Japan's MITI began negotiating to address the industry's trade complaints. The USTR acted as a loyal representative of the semiconductor industry's position. Abandoning its customary opposition to managed-trade agreements, the USTR aggressively pursued the industry's agenda of regulating Japanese import purchases and export prices. In fact, as Douglas Irwin recounts, "SIA representatives were often in an adjacent room, available for close consultations during the negotiations and ready to advise USTR about what was acceptable and what was not."[1]

After several months of contentious negotiations, the two countries reached an agreement on September 2, 1986. This agreement effectively created an international semiconductor cartel that continues to fix export prices and countries' market shares artificially. While the cartel agreement was initially heralded as a breakthrough and model for future U.S.-Japan dispute resolution, in practice the agreement backfired. The cartel has been extremely costly to U.S. consumers and the U.S. semiconductor industry, and highly profitable to Japanese companies. As economists David Mowery and Nathan Rosenberg state, "If the Semiconductor Agreement...is an example of successful 'managed trade,' it is hard to know what might constitute a failure."[2] The sections following review the disappointing results of the cartel agreement's market-sharing and price-fixing terms.

Fixing Market Shares

Despite the Reagan administration's general aversion to industrial policy, the United States sought a firm commitment from Japan that U.S. semiconductor imports would grow to at least 20 percent of the market by 1991. To achieve this target, Japan pledged to "encourage Japanese users to purchase more foreign-based semiconductors and to provide further support for expanded sales by foreign capital-affiliated semiconductor firms in Japan."[3] These goals were to be met "through the establishment of an organization to provide sales assistance for foreign capital-affiliated semiconductor companies and through promotion of long-term relationships between Japanese semiconductor purchasers and foreign capital-affiliated semiconductor companies." In practice, this meant that MITI would pressure Japanese chip buyers to shift their purchases toward U.S. sources.

Both governments denied that they were setting an explicit market share target—in fact, the 20 percent share was mentioned only in a "secret" side-letter to the 1986 cartel agreement, a ploy that was designed to allow both countries to maintain their public commitment to the principles of free trade. Privately, however, both governments were under strong political pressure to reach the 20 percent target. U.S. semiconductor firms had attracted powerful political allies in both Congress and the administration.

These allies placed pressure on the USTR negotiators, who in turn exerted pressure on their Japanese counterparts to accept specific market share goals. The era of managed-trade policy was ushered in.

How successful was the cartel agreement at meeting its market access target? When the agreement was signed, U.S. semiconductor firms had an 8.6 percent share of the Japanese market. By the third quarter of 1991, that share had risen to 14.3 percent.[4] Thus, the agreement produced only half the desired 12 percent increase in U.S. market share. More important than their failure to meet an arbitrary numerical target, American firms also failed to achieve the desired structural change in Japanese buying relationships. American firms proved largely unsuccessful at establishing customer-supplier relationships with Japanese computer manufacturers, relationships that would have signaled a long-term shift in market access. Instead, most of the industry's increased market share came from spot market purchases by major Japanese semiconductor producers, who were under stiff political pressure to meet the 1991 targets agreed to by MITI.[5]

Why were U.S. market access gains relatively meager? U.S. semiconductor firms claim that the Japanese government failed to exert adequate pressure on computer electronics manufacturers to "buy American." According to this view, it was not that market share targeting had failed, it was that Japanese bureaucrats had undermined the policy before it had a chance to succeed. It is naïve, however, to attribute the poor track record of U.S. firms solely to Japanese government policies. Economist Thomas Pugel notes that "Japanese buyers generally perceive U.S. [semiconductor] devices to be of lower quality and reliability than Japanese devices and U.S. firms to be less reliable in delivery, less helpful with technical services, and less willing to redesign products and renegotiate agreements."[6] Quality and marketing concerns limited sales by U.S. firms.

Chip manufacturers such as Motorola and Texas Instruments that met Japanese quality and reliability demands *were* successful in penetrating the Japanese market. In the late 1980s, these and other successful U.S. suppliers added sales offices, design centers, and testing facilities in Japan to provide on-site marketing and quality control. These investments paid off handsomely in semiconductor sales and profits.[7] Success also came to firms that formed technology-sharing and marketing alliances with Japanese counterparts. Motorola's far-reaching alliance with Toshiba was instrumental in allowing the company to gain a strong foothold in the Japanese DRAM market just two years after Motorola had withdrawn from DRAM production altogether.

What were the costs of the industry's small gains in market share? First, the United States was forced to exert considerable political pressure on an important ally. The dispute over semiconductors spilled far beyond just this one industry to poison trade relations between the United States and Japan in a wide range of high-technology and other sectors. Second, the United States effectively abandoned its long-standing commitment to noninterventionist trade and industrial policies by acquiescing to industry demands that an explicit numerical target be set. This opened the door to the demands of countless other industries, including telecommunications and pharmaceuticals, for market access guarantees.

Finally, the cartel agreement had the unintended effect of encouraging the resurgence of MITI. The Japanese planning agency was directly involved in the agreement's negotiation and, as explained in the next section, played an active role in overseeing the cartel's administration. It is ironic that this resurgence was the direct product of U.S. policy makers' wanting less MITI intervention, yet at the same time demanding more control over the buying practices of Japanese firms. Kenneth Flamm, often a supporter of activist policies in semiconductor trade, himself acknowledges the contradiction in U.S. policy makers' position:

The U.S. semiconductor industry cannot have it both ways. If American chip makers genuinely want the U.S. government to insist that MITI's postwar role as the administrative guide of the Japanese industry has no place in the market-driven high-tech trading system of the 1990s, and continue to push for structural change within Japan, they cannot at the same time promote an agenda that implicitly strengthens the system of informal, behind the scenes, quasi-legal guidance they have condemned.[8]

Fixing a Cartel Price

The second component of the cartel agreement established a minimum price or "price floor" for semiconductors exported from Japan. This provision grew directly from the SIA's charges that Japanese semiconductor firms had been selling at below-cost prices in the U.S. market to gain market share and, eventually, to drive American competitors from the industry. A primary goal of the SIA was to prevent future outbreaks of dumping. To this end, the cartel agreement stipulated that an elaborate system would be created by the U.S. and Japanese governments to monitor and control Japanese semiconductor export prices. The U.S. Department of Commerce established "fair market values" (FMVs) for each Japanese semiconductor firm. While the FMVs were nominally tied to accounting estimates of production costs of Japanese firms, in practice they were arbitrary and economically nonsensical. These FMVs established a price floor for firms. If a firm exported at prices below the FMV, it would be presumed to have "dumped" by selling below its costs of production. To enforce these FMV pricing rules, MITI agreed to monitor the export prices of Japanese firms for a wide range of semiconductor products. These prices, together with estimates of production costs of individual Japanese firms, were then regularly reported to the Department of Commerce for comparison against the FMVs.

What effects did the cartel price floor have on the industry? First, U.S. computer manufacturers paid sharply higher prices for chips, prices that eventually were passed onto U.S. consumers. By one conservative estimate, the price floor amounted to an annual tax of $500–600 million on U.S. computer buyers.[9] Immediately after the cartel agreement was signed, prices of semiconductors imported from Japan jumped sharply. U.S. purchasers reported paying prices for 256K DRAMs that were between two and eight times the prices they were paying before the cartel.[10] But the SIA was not content with even these unprecedented price hikes. The industry association was convinced that Japanese producers were violating the cartel agreement by selling at below-FMV prices in Europe and the Far East. The association claimed that smuggling from these lower-priced markets into the United States was widespread and threatened to undermine the cartel agreement's intent to boost prices.[11]

Acting on industry complaints and faced with organized political pressure in Congress, in April 1987 the Reagan administration imposed retaliatory tariffs of 100 percent on a range of Japanese computers and electronic goods. Japanese bureaucrats quickly got the message, and they pressured chip manufacturers to raise their export prices still further.[12] Once again, U.S. chip users were the victims. By 1988, chip prices had soared to unprecedented levels. Over a four-month period that year, spot market prices for 256K DRAMs tripled. Chip users also experienced delays and rationing. Widespread shortages developed as Japanese firms cut back on production, and U.S. computer manufacturers reported frequent difficulties in obtaining adequate supplies at *any* price. Japanese suppliers began rationing chips, and supply shortages forced American computer makers to delay the introduction of new models. In contrast, the Japanese, who were not subjected to these artificial shortages and inflated prices, forged ahead.[13]

A second costly consequence of the cartel's price floor was that it made Japanese chip manufacturers even *more* productive. By 1987, all but two of the major U.S. manufacturers of DRAMs had withdrawn from production.[14] The cartel agreement did not spark reentry by U.S. producers into the DRAM market. Thus, while cartel-mandated production cutbacks in Japan did help boost DRAM prices, only a small share of the resulting profits found their way back to American DRAM producers. Higher profits instead went to Japanese chip manufacturers who commanded the lion's share of the world DRAM market. By one estimate, higher chip prices raised Japanese firms' annual profits by $3–4 billion.[15]

Japanese firms plowed these windfall earnings back into research and development for future chip generations. The result was that

> the gap between capital and R&D spending by Japanese companies and American companies expanded still further. By 1988 capital spending by Japanese semiconductor companies was nearly $2 billion more than that of American semiconductor companies, and the R&D spending of the top five Japanese companies exceeded that of the top five American merchant firms by about $1.5 billion. Thus, the bubble profits had the perverse result of strengthening the Japanese companies for future rounds of competition in new products.[16]

A final consequence of the price floors and monitoring system was to facilitate collusion among Japanese chip manufacturers. MITI's intervention—mandated by U.S. policy makers—amounted to creating a cartel among Japanese semiconductor producers. MITI established a committee to meet with semiconductor producers to review their production plans for the coming quarter and to set industry targets to avoid "overproduction" that could lower export prices. In a series of steps beginning in early 1987, MITI lowered firms' production targets, which led market prices to rise sharply. Once MITI had taught the industry how to act as a cartel, Japanese firms eagerly abandoned competition over market shares.

In sum, the semiconductor cartel agreement provides one of the clearest examples of targeting gone awry. The agreement's intended beneficiaries—U.S. chip manufacturers—gained little from inflated chip prices because most of them had already abandoned the market. The agreement's unintended victims—U.S. chip buyers—suffered from drastically higher prices and acute supply shortages. And the policy also produced an unintended beneficiary—Japanese producers, who earned windfall profits and were emboldened by government intervention to behave like an industry cartel and further exploit their market power.

Renewing the Cartel

The original cartel agreement signed in 1986 was scheduled to expire by July 1991. Economists and representatives from the computer industry strongly opposed extending the cartel's lifespan. They argued that the cartel agreement had produced little tangible benefit to U.S. chip manufacturers and had cost U.S. consumers millions of dollars from higher prices for computers and other electronic products. But pressure from semiconductor industry lobbyists ultimately prevailed, and after another round of negotiations in 1991, Japan and the United States reached a new five-year accord on price and market share targets.

The 1991 cartel effectively institutionalized government micromanagement of the chip industry. Whereas in 1986 the two governments had attempted to keep secret their agreement to set a 20 percent market share target for U.S. firms in Japan, in 1991 the quotas became a center- piece of the accord. The renewed agreement explicitly stated that the 20 percent target should be reached by the fourth quarter of 1992. To reach this target, Japan announced a series of "emergency measures" designed to pressure the country's ten largest semiconductor users to commit to increasing their American chip purchases.[17] To bolster this pressure, the U.S. government made it known that it stood ready to retaliate if the market share target was not reached on time.

Faced with internal political pressure and the threat of foreign retaliation, Japanese chip users gradually increased their U.S. purchases. In the fourth quarter of 1992, the arbitrary target was reached when the U.S. market share rose to 20.2 percent, although this share later slipped to 19 percent, then to 19.2 percent, and then to 18.1 percent in the first three quarters of 1993.[18] Did this represent a "success" for the U.S. industry or a validation of managed-trade policy? The answer is no. The transitory rise in U.S. market share resulted from a modest rise in Japanese purchases of foreign chips coupled with a contraction in the total market for semiconductors in Japan. In other words, the Japanese recession of 1991–1992 contributed as much to raising the U.S. market share as did the combined pressures of political bargaining and government mandates.

The 1991 cartel extension is a classic example of exactly how difficult it is to extricate the government once it launches an interventionist initiative. To gain political support for market share quotas, the SIA had originally promised that "after a 20 percent level had been achieved, [the U.S.] share would float to an appropriate level based on competitive merit and without further government targets...[the target was] a threshold from which market forces would then take over and operate."[19] But once the arbitrary 20 percent target was reached, the industry association quickly reversed its position to urge that the market share quota be maintained, if not increased. As Brink Lindsey concludes from the semiconductor case, "Nothing lasts forever, but 'temporary' federal assistance comes close. Whenever government does intervene in an industry, there is almost irresistible pressure for it to remain there. Not only do beneficiaries within the industry become addicted to government support, but bureaucrats become convinced that the industry can't run without them."[20]

The cartel's extension also effectively institutionalized U.S. government regulation of semiconductor prices. The setting of fair market values for Japanese chip export prices was originally proposed as a temporary solution to the problem of Japanese dumping. On its face, the 1991 agreement appeared to relax the price floors set by the United States to curb dumping. In reality, the agreement continued to require Japan to collect data on prices, costs, and production from all its semiconductor firms. These data are to be made available to the U.S. government in the event that future antidumping charges are brought against Japanese producers. Thus, the message to Japanese firms remains as clear as before: produce too much or export at too low a price, and you will be subjected to immediate sanctions under U.S. antidumping laws. The history of arbitrary and politically charged treatment of Japanese firms under U.S. antidumping laws serves as a constant reminder that politics rather than economics drives American semiconductor policy.[21]

Managed Trade Spreads

History almost repeated itself when South Korea emerged in the early 1990s as a major competitor in the DRAM market. Korean manufacturers quickly attracted the attention of U.S. firms and policy makers. In April 1992, Micron Technologies—the same firm that used the antidumping laws against seven Japanese rivals in 1985—

filed an antidumping petition charging that Korean firms were exporting DRAMs at below-cost prices. In a virtual repeat of the earlier antidumping investigations against Japanese suppliers, the Commerce Department levied preliminary fines ranging as high as 87 percent against three Korean manufacturers: Goldstar, Hyundai, and Samsung.[22] Micron also convinced the Commerce Department to levy fines on imported computer subassemblies (such as circuitry boards) that used Korean chips. This move prompted at least one large U.S. computer manufacturer, AST Research, to consider moving its production overseas to avoid the drastically higher costs. AST estimated that the higher duties would force it to move 700 U.S. production jobs overseas.[23]

The Korean semiconductor industry faced a golden opportunity, much as Japanese firms did in 1986. Sensing that the Clinton administration would eagerly embrace a managed-trade agreement modeled after the 1986–1991 U.S.-Japan cartel, the Korean industry association and government proposed a similar plan in January 1993. In exchange for U.S. suspension of the antidumping case, Korean firms promised to monitor the price of their semiconductor exports to the United States in an industry cartel arrangement. The Korean government also promised to boost imports of U.S. semiconductors by putting pressure on chip buyers and reducing import barriers. Accepting slightly higher imports was viewed as a small investment that promised the substantial return of boosting Korean export profits through a government-enforced cartel agreement.

In the end, Korea and the United States never signed an agreement. But this temporary halt in the spread of managed trade provides little reassurance about long-term trends. The Korean proposal was rejected *not* because managed trade had been discredited in the eyes of policy makers. Instead, it was rejected by Micron, which thought that high antidumping penalties would provide the best protection against Korean competition. Micron also expected that it would gain little from the Korean proposal to liberalize its import market. Because Micron had been the driving force behind the antidumping cases, the U.S. government deferred to its wishes and rejected the Korean proposal. Ironically, in May 1993 the Commerce Department revised its preliminary antidumping fines drastically downward, depriving Micron of much of its anticipated protection from Korean firms.[24] Micron's ultimate disappointment with antidumping protection may encourage semiconductor firms and the Clinton administration to embrace managed-trade agreements even more readily in the future.

8

The Sematech Experiment

Sematech, the Semiconductor Manufacturing Technology Corporation, is another example of "temporary" government intervention that became a permanent fixture on the political landscape, despite its having provided few measurable benefits. Sematech was established in 1987 amid concerns that Japanese semiconductor firms were outspending and outperforming their American competitors in research on manufacturing processes. These concerns were fueled by a National Science Foundation report that concluded that Japanese chip manufacturers were technologically superior in both optical and X-ray lithography. To reverse this trend, fourteen U.S. semiconductor firms formed the Sematech consortium under the auspices of the 1984 National Cooperative Research Act, which granted antitrust immunity to research joint ventures. The firms lobbied for and won matching funds from the federal government, a subsidy that has totaled $100 million annually. The original government commitment was to underwrite Sematech for five years, after which member firms would fully fund their joint research projects. In 1993, however, Congress again renewed Sematech's matching subsidies.

Sematech has recently announced that it will end its reliance on public funds in 1997, although it has made no moves in this direction. Does Sematech's announcement disprove Brink Lindsey's rule that "nothing lasts forever, but 'temporary' federal assistance comes close"? No. Sematech plans to continue to bid for federal funds on specific projects, even as it declines annual subsidy appropriations.[1] More important, Sematech's recent announcement was driven more by political realities than by underlying economics. Sematech realized that it faced an uphill battle to convince Congress to extend subsidies beyond 1997, in light of its dismal track record in manufacturing research. Thus, publicly declining subsidies came at little real cost to the consortium. Indeed, announcing that it was weaning itself from federal subsidies gave Sematech considerable public relations capital. Eventually, Sematech backers are likely to want to cash in this public relations capital to ask once again for federal sponsorship.

Sematech forms an integral part of the Clinton administration's strategy to use activist technology policy and industry-government cooperatives to improve U.S. manufacturing competitiveness. A White House press release touted Sematech's suitability "as a model for federal consortia funded to advance other critical technologies."[2] Economist Paul Romer cites Sematech as a prototype for high-technology research partnerships as part of a general national technology strategy.[3] Sematech's backers promise widespread economic benefits from government-supported cooperative research. For the semiconductor industry, Sematech was supposed to reestablish U.S. firms once again as world leaders in manufacturing technologies. Sematech envisaged a five-year plan to achieve parity with Japan by 1991 and regain world leadership by 1993.[4] For the rest of the economy, Sematech was supposed to provide positive spillovers. A Congressional Budget Office Report argued that "since semiconductors now have so many applications, [semiconductor industry] cost reductions should be spread throughout the economy. If Sematech achieves its goals, the nation would benefit both from the better quality and lower cost of semiconductors the industry produces and from the incorporation of these devices in the products of other industries."[5]

Has Sematech fulfilled these promises? Unfortunately, the answer is no. Sematech has failed to raise research spending of semiconductor firms, their productivity, or their profitability. Reflecting these failures, Sematech's membership has gradually dwindled. The government consortium has also been forced to radically refocus its efforts away from cutting-edge research, because American equipment manufacturers were unable to supply state-of-the-art machinery. Sematech's revised mission is now much less glamorous: propping up the declining U.S. semiconductor manufacturing equipment industry. This section explains that Sematech's poor record is also attributable to its having stifled the firms' entrepreneurship and its lack of direct manufacturing experience. The costs of Sematech transcend the government subsidies paid for by taxpayers: Sematech has also undermined U.S. legitimacy in opposing foreign governments' industrial policies and has encouraged the U.S. semiconductor industry to become insular and protective.

Expectations

Initial planning for Sematech envisaged that member firms would manufacture DRAMs for sale. Actual manufacturing experience was thought to be an essential ingredient for developing state-of-the-art manufacturing techniques. For two reasons, this plan was rejected even before Sematech began operating. First, chip manufacturers that remained outside of Sematech strenuously objected that a manufacturing consortium would stiffen the competition that they faced. Second, and more ominous for the consortium's prospects, IBM feared that as the largest member of the consortium, it would be forced to buy Sematech chips if other buyers could not be found. Sematech therefore adopted the more limited goal of encouraging cooperative research, the results of which member firms could then incorporate into their own manufacturing operations.

In an attempt to ensure that its research would be useful to all member firms, Sematech originally focused on generic, "precompetitive" research into manufacturing processes. According to the president of Sematech, William J. Spencer, the consortium's focus on generic research would "potentially benefit all members without threatening their core proprietary capabilities."[6] Consistent with this goal, one of Sematech's first projects was to develop new manufacturing processes that would allow much narrower circuitry lines to be etched onto silicon wafers. Narrower lines would allow more circuits to be put on a given sized chip, and the additional circuits would dramatically expand the chip's memory capacity. To meet this ambitious goal, Sematech "was to purchase [chip manufacturing] equipment and establish a leading-edge wafer processing facility. Information gained concerning the performance of manufacturing equipment, and ways of optimizing the construction and operation of the fabrication line, would be transferred back to member firms."[7] According to Spencer, this strategy of centralizing funding and testing would "lower the costs of equipment development and introduction by reducing the duplication of firms' efforts to develop and quantify new tools."[8] Even at Sematech's initiation, however, these expectations and goals remained the subject of heated internal debate. Economists Peter Grindley, David Mowery, and Brian Silverman note that Sematech members "questioned whether the development of advanced manufacturing processes was an appropriate objective for an industry consortium."[9]

Realities

How do the expectations and the reality of Sematech match up? Sematech proponents label the experiment a success. Favorable reviews claim that "Sematech is demonstrating

that federal industrial policy—under the right circumstances—can be highly effective," and policy activists credit
Sematech with "saving [the] U.S. industry's place in semiconductor manufacturing."[10] Hyperbole aside, neither of
these claims can be substantiated by Sematech's actual
performance. Sematech has fallen prey to exactly the same
pitfalls that undermined previous industrial policy experiments. In the words of Cyrix Semiconductor President Jerry
Rogers, "Sematech has spent five years and $1 billion but
there are still no measurable benefits to the industry."[11]

Almost from the beginning, the reality of Sematech
began to diverge from proponents' expectations. When
Sematech started its project of narrowing circuitry lines
on silicon wafers, it began experimenting with line widths
of 0.8 microns. To help get Sematech off and running,
IBM donated its designs and proprietary technology for 4
megabit DRAMs and AT&T contributed technology for its
64 kilobit SRAM (static random access memory). With this
assistance, Sematech was to meet its preliminary goal in
1989 of developing manufacturing processes for 0.8 micron chips. But other chip manufacturers—including some
U.S. firms that had chosen not to join Sematech—had already been selling 0.8 micron chips since 1986. As Brink
Lindsey summarizes, "Sematech was able to borrow technology from private companies and reproduce manufacturing results that other private companies had achieved
years before—and do it with taxpayers' money."[12]

Sematech's next setback came just two years into its
operations, when the consortium was transformed from a
research joint venture into a bailout for U.S. semiconductor equipment manufacturers. Sematech was unable to
avoid this transformation, because the declining U.S. equipment industry had been unable to manufacture the state-
of-the-art machines necessary for chip manufacturers to
regain international technological leadership. Reflecting
the dramatic shift in its priorities, between 1989 and 1990
Sematech's annual expenditures for experimenting with

manufacturing techniques plummeted from $119 million to $45 million. At the same time, Sematech's bailout to equipment suppliers rose from just $30 million in 1989 to $130 million in 1991, representing more than half of Sematech's total budget.[13] By abandoning its original agenda, Sematech implicitly acknowledged that the consortium would be unable to meet its objective of regaining leadership in semiconductor manufacturing technology.

Sematech has also managed to back more than its share of losers, because it has not been subject to the market discipline faced by private investors. As part of its new strategy to bail out U.S. equipment manufacturers, Sematech invested heavily in two firms, GCA and Silicon Valley Group Lithography (SVGL).[14] By 1990, GCA and SVGL were the only two U.S. companies that could supply advanced photolithographic machines to chip manufacturers. By subsidizing the operations of the financially troubled firms, Sematech hoped to retain a secure supply of state-of-the-art manufacturing equipment for member firms. Despite making a series of important advances in photolithographic technology, however—and despite receiving more than $60 million in direct subsidies from Sematech—GCA never became profitable. In early 1993, its parent company (General Signal) was forced to close the firm's doors.

With the aid of a $30 million direct subsidy from Sematech, SVGL made several technological breakthroughs in lithographic equipment. Like GCA, however, the discoveries never proved profitable because demand from U.S. chip manufacturers for the equipment remained weak. To solve its cash flow problems, SVGL negotiated a ten-year technology-development partnership with one of its major *Japanese* competitors. Canon obtained exclusive rights to sell SVGL machines in Japan and much of the rest of Asia. As *The Economist* notes, "Sematech's continuing support for SVGL is a way for American taxpayers to subsidize a rival semiconductor equipment maker in Japan."[15]

The combination of unrealized goals, shifting priorities, and costly bailouts has made Sematech a resounding disappointment. Economists Douglas Irwin and Peter Klenow have measured Sematech's performance by a series of economic yardsticks, and they find that the consortium has consistently come up short.[16] From a survey of five Sematech members, three firms said that the consortium had not at all changed their total R&D spending—meaning that research by Sematech was offset dollar-for-dollar by reductions in their in-house research. The other two firms surveyed said that Sematech had actually caused them to *lower* their total research budget. When questioned by the General Accounting Office in 1992, all but two Sematech members said they were unwilling to increase their funding for the research consortium.[17]

Irwin and Klenow also found that Sematech did not raise member firms' returns on assets, did not raise firms' investment-to-sales or investment-to-assets ratios, and did not have any appreciable effect on industry productivity. Given this dismal report, it is not surprising that Sematech's membership has dwindled. Three of the consortium's original fourteen members have dropped out, and another four have indicated that they intend to leave soon.[18] Irwin and Klenow reported that "all of the former members questioned the...direction of Sematech's research effort...[and] stated that their own internal R&D spending has been more productive than investments in Sematech."[19]

Why Was Sematech Unsuccessful?

Why has Sematech largely failed to meet its goals? There appear to be several reasons. First, Sematech was devoid of the entrepreneurial spirit that through the 1970s had made the U.S. semiconductor industry the world's leader in manufacturing process research. Sematech's rules, dues structure, and research agenda favored older, more established companies over innovative start-ups. It is not surprising, therefore, that many of the most successful small chip manufacturers such as Altera, Cirrus Logic, Cypress Semiconductor, and Xilinx have steadfastly refused to join Sematech. Brink Lindsey likens Sematech to a "clique of large, established, high profile companies using government money to fend off not just foreign competition but also up-and-coming rivals here at home."[20] Lindsey continues,

> Buzzwords like *precompetitive* notwithstanding, Sematech is yet another example of government meddling in an industry to pick winners and losers. And as usual, the bureaucrats have backed the wrong horse. Within the sunrise industry of microelectronics, the government has managed to locate and subsidize sunset companies to the detriment of those young and dynamic companies that represent the industry's future.[21]

T. J. Rodgers, president of the highly successful start-up firm Cypress Semiconductor, puts it more bluntly: "Consortia are formed by people who have lost."[22]

Second, Sematech's early decision not to produce commercial chips deprived the consortium of crucial manufacturing experience through learning by doing. According to Rodgers, this was a fatal mistake: "There's no one in this business who believes you can go down the learning curve without manufacturing. But Sematech's kickoff charter, approved by Congress, was to learn without manufacturing. It was a preposterous charter, and I said so at the time."[23] This lack of vision has continued to plague Sematech since its birth. As market conditions changed, Sematech was forced to alter its charter objectives continually, each time moving further and further away from the manufacturing technology frontier. When even the consortium's own members cannot define a coherent research and business strategy, it is little surprise that

71

Sematech wound up disappointing many of its strongest backers in Congress.[24]

The Costs of Sematech

If Sematech had merely failed at its mission of restoring U.S. competitiveness in semiconductor manufacturing technology, it would have represented simply a poor investment of public funds. Unfortunately, the costs imposed by this industrial policy experiment were considerably greater. Government-industry partnerships like Sematech undermine the long-stated opposition of the United States to large-scale technology development subsidies that other governments have bestowed on programs such as Europe's Airbus. Sematech thus represents one step down a slippery slope. As the difference between U.S. and foreign technology programs narrows, we erode our authority to oppose such subsidies in this country and our ability to persuade trading partners to abandon their own subsidies for high-technology industries.

A second cost imposed by Sematech comes from its mercantilist approach to research and technology sharing. Sematech steadfastly refused to allow non-U.S. firms to join its ranks and has often sought to block joint ventures between members and Japanese partners. In an era of multinational corporations and proliferating research joint ventures, erecting strict technology barriers is simply bad policy. It denies American firms the scientific and manufacturing advances that many of their foreign competitors develop and acquire. Economists David Mowery and Nathan Rosenberg warn that if Sematech's "mercantilist philosophy...spreads more widely within U.S. science and technology policy, the results could be detrimental to the strength of the U.S. science and technology base."[25]

9
Looking to the Future

The futility of industrial policy in sector after sector has apparently not shaken the faith of targeting's most vocal proponents. The United States is now poised to embark on another industrial policy experiment, this time in flat panel displays (FPDs). To rally political support, targeting proponents have announced that they regard the FPD industry as strategic to U.S. defense capabilities and international competitiveness. Like semiconductors, the U.S. FPD industry is being portrayed as if its very existence is at stake. Laura Tyson warns ominously that "advanced display technology was an American invention, but Japanese companies dominate its commercial applications. Only a handful of small American firms remain in the business."[1] Another Clinton economic adviser, Bowman Cutler, argues that "we need to establish a business base [and to create] a model of technological development that will equip U.S. companies to break into markets already seized by Japanese concerns."[2]

The rhetoric surrounding FPDs is reminiscent of the rhetoric during the semiconductor targeting episode. American policies bear a disturbing resemblance to those that were applied—and that backfired—in the semiconductor industry. In July 1991, the Advanced Display Manufacturers of America industry association won an antidumping suit against its Japanese rivals. As a result of the suit, a 63 percent antidumping tax was levied on computer screens imported from Japan. Computer manufacturers were forced to pay sharply higher prices for screens, just as they had a few years earlier when antidumping fines were imposed on DRAMs. The consequences of this protectionist policy are predictable: harming U.S. industries using FPDs as inputs and encouraging them to migrate to lower-cost production locations abroad.

FPD research policy is also repeating the mistakes from the semiconductor industry and is going one large step further. In August 1992, the Defense Department's Advanced Research Projects Agency unveiled a plan to establish and fund a research consortium of U.S. firms to refine manufacturing techniques for the next generation of display screens. The initiative is far more ambitious and interventionist than Sematech. In early 1995, the administration raised the stakes by promising to devote up to $500 million over the next decade to encourage U.S. firms to build FPD factories. As Claude Barfield of the American Enterprise Institute writes, the new initiative commits the government to the Herculean "task of creating and managing a private market for a fledgling technology until it reaches maturity."[3] Given the government's failed record of intervention in existing industries, the prospects for government's "masterminding the creation of an entire *new* industry" are much more glum. Indeed, the government's own Office of Technology Assessment (OTA) rates the chances of Washington's successfully building a flat panel display industry from scratch as "dismal." The OTA recently warned that the project would "require massive investments in the neighborhood of half a billion dollars per plant, and by no means ensure the United States a significant presence in this industry."[4]

Rather than attempt to manipulate markets, trade and industrial policy should focus on liberalizing private markets. The recent Uruguay GATT Agreement provides a blueprint for countries to reject inward-looking, *dirigiste* policies in favor of free markets. The Uruguay agreement continues progress in lowering tariff and nontariff barriers, strengthening enforcement of free trade rules, and controlling the spread of subsidies in high-technology industries. Agreements among nations to rely more on private market forces, and less on government edict, offer the best insurance against future trade and industrial policy wars. They also offer the most promise for worldwide prosperity and economic growth.

Notes

CHAPTER 1: INTRODUCTION

1. Jagdish N. Bhagwati, *Protectionism* (Cambridge: MIT Press, 1988), pp. 4–9.

CHAPTER 2: WHY HAS TARGETING GAINED AN AUDIENCE?

1. Karl Zinsmeister, "MITI Mouse: Japan's Industrial Policy Doesn't Work," *Policy Review* (Spring 1993), p. 30.

2. Laura D'Andrea Tyson, *Who's Bashing Whom? Trade Conflict in High Technology Industries* (Washington, D.C.: Institute for International Economics, 1992), p. 1.

CHAPTER 3: TARGETING IN THEORY AND PRACTICE

1. Paul R. Krugman, "Targeted Industrial Policies: Theory and Evidence," in Dominick Salvatore, ed., *The New Protectionist Threat to World Welfare* (New York: North-Holland, 1987), pp. 266–96.

2. Paul R. Krugman, "The U.S. Response to Foreign Industrial Targeting," *Brookings Papers on Economic Activity*, vol. 1 (1984), pp. 116–18.

3. Kozo Yamamura, "Caveat Emptor: The Industrial Policy of Japan," in Paul R. Krugman, ed., *Strategic Trade Policy and the New International Economics* (Cambridge: MIT Press, 1986), pp. 169–209.

4. Andrew R. Dick, "Does Import Protection Act as Export Promotion? Evidence from the United States," *Oxford Economic Papers*, vol. 46, no. 1 (January 1994), pp. 83–101.

5. Anne O. Krueger and Baran Tuncer, "An Empirical Test of the Infant Industry Argument," *American Economic Review*, vol. 72, no. 5 (December 1982), pp. 1142–52.

6. Semiconductor Industry Association, *The Effect of Government Targeting on World Semiconductor Competition* (Cupertino, Calif.: Semiconductor Industry Association, 1983).

7. Ibid., p. 59.

8. Sematech's track record is reviewed at greater length in chapter 8.

9. P. D. Henderson, "Two British Errors: Their Probable Size and Some Possible Lessons," *Oxford Economic Papers*, vol. 29, no. 2 (July 1977), pp. 159–205.

10. Tyson, *Who's Bashing Whom?* p. 35.

11. Gary C. Hufbauer et al., *Trade Protection in the United States: 31 Case Studies* (Washington, D.C.: Institute for International Economics, 1986), pp. 14–15.

12. Robert M. Uriu, "The Declining Industries of Japan: Adjustment and Reallocation," *Journal of International Affairs,* vol. 38 (Summer 1984), pp. 99–111; and Zinsmeister, "MITI Mouse."

13. Katsuro Sakoh, "Japan's Economic Success: Industrial Policy of Free Market?" *Cato Journal,* vol. 4, no. 2 (Fall 1984), pp. 521–47.

14. Chalmers Johnson, *MITI and the Japanese Miracle* (Stanford: Stanford University Press, 1982); Clyde V. Prestowitz, *Trading Places: How America Allowed Japan to Take the Lead* (Tokyo: Charles E. Tuttle Co., 1988); and Yamamura, "Caveat Emptor."

15. Andrew R. Dick, "The Competitive Consequences of Japan's Export Cartel Associations," *Journal of the Japanese and International Economies*, vol. 6, no. 3 (September 1992), pp. 275–98.

16. David E. Weinstein, "Administrative Guidance and Cartels in Japan (1957–1988): Did MITI Really Coordinate Japanese Industry?" Harvard Institute of Economic Research discussion paper 1628, February 1993.

17. Zinsmeister, "MITI Mouse," p. 33.

18. Quoted in ibid., pp. 33–34.

19. David R. Henderson, "The Myth of MITI," *Fortune*, August 8, 1983, pp. 113–16.

20. Quoted in Charles L. Schultze, "Industrial Policy: A Dissent," *Brookings Review* (Fall 1983), pp. 3–12.

21. David R. Henderson, "Japan and the Myth of MITI," in David Henderson, ed., *The Fortune Encyclopedia of Economics* (New York: Warner, 1993), pp. 743–46.

22. Sakoh, "Japan's Economic Success," p. 541.

23. Ibid.

24. H. Don B. H. Gunasekera and Rod Tyers, "Imperfect Competition and Returns to Scale in a Newly Industrializing Economy: A General Equilibrium Analysis of Korean Trade Policy," *Journal of Development Economics*, vol. 34, nos. 1/2 (November 1990), pp. 223–47.

25. Danny M. Leipziger and Peter A. Petri, "Korean Industrial Policy," World Bank discussion paper 197, 1993.

CHAPTER 4: WHY HAS TARGETING FAILED?

1. Keith Cowling and Dennis C. Mueller, "The Social Cost of Monopoly Power," *Economic Journal*, vol. 88 (December 1978), pp. 724–48.

2. See F. M. Scherer and David Ross, *Industrial Market Structure and Economic Performance* (Boston: Houghton Mifflin, 1990), for numerical evidence on low entry barriers in a wide range of manufacturing industries.

3. John J. Lazlo, Jr., *The Japanese Semiconductor Industry* (San Francisco: Hambrecht and Quist, 1985), pp. 14–15.

4. J. T. Norman, "Bulk of U.S. Imports Are Said to Be Shipments between Firms," *Wall Street Journal*, October 15, 1990; and U.S. Department of Commerce, *Survey of Current Business*, January 1990, p. B11.

5. David P. Angel, *Restructuring for Innovation: The Remaking of the U.S. Semiconductor Industry* (New York: Guilford Press, 1994), pp. 160–61.

6. Andrew R. Dick, "Strategic Trade Policy and Welfare: The Empirical Consequences of Cross-Ownership," *Journal of International Economics*, vol. 35, nos. 3/4 (November 1993), pp. 227–49.

7. Robert E. Baldwin and Richard K. Green, "The Effects of Protection on Domestic Output," in R.E. Baldwin, ed., *Trade Policy Issues and Empirical Analysis* (Chicago: University of Chicago Press, 1988), pp. 205–26; and Hufbauer et al., *Trade Protection in the United States*.

8. Richard Marston, "Pricing to Market in Japanese Manufacturing," *Journal of International Economics*, vol. 80, no. 5 (December 1990), pp. 217–36.

9. Bee Y. Aw and Mark J. Roberts, "Measuring Quality Change in Quota-constrained Import Markets," *Journal of International Economics*, vol. 21, nos. 1/2 (August 1986), pp. 45–60.

10. John R. Baldwin and Paul K. Gorecki, "Trade, Tariffs and Relative Plant Scale in Canadian Manufacturing Industries: 1970–1979," Discussion paper 232, 1983, Economic Council of Canada, Ottawa; and John R. Baldwin and Paul K. Gorecki, *The Role of Scale in Canada–U.S. Productivity Differences in the Manufacturing Sector: 1970–1979* (Toronto: University of Toronto Press, 1986).

11. Dynamic random access memories, which are silicon chips that store information electronically.

12. Sakoh, "Japan's Economic Success," p. 527.

13. Allan H. Meltzer, "Why Governments Make Bad Venture Capitalists," *Wall Street Journal*, May 5, 1993.

14. Schultze, "Industrial Policy," pp. 9–10.

15. Ibid., p. 10.

CHAPTER 5: SEMICONDUCTORS—NO EXCEPTION

1. Tyson, *Who's Bashing Whom?* p. 86.

2. Andrew Grove, "How Intel Makes Spending Take Off: Interview," *Fortune*, February 22, 1993, p. 57.

3. Michael Borrus, Laura D'Andrea Tyson, and John Zysman, "Creating Advantage: How Government Policies Shape International Trade in the Semiconductor Industry," in Paul Krugman, ed., *Strategic Trade Policy and the New International Economics* (Cambridge: MIT Press, 1986), pp. 91–113.

4. Angel, *Restructuring for Innovation*, pp. 157–58.

5. For a brief history of early U.S. government support in the semiconductor industry, see Tyson, *Who's Bashing Whom?* pp. 80–90.

6. Federal Interagency Staff Working Group, *The Semiconductor Industry* (Washington, D.C.: National Science Foundation, 1987), p. 31.

7. Only beginning in the late 1980s did the Japanese share of U.S. chip demand rise sharply.

8. Brink Lindsey, "Don't Renew the Semiconductor Cartel," *Wall Street Journal*, May 20, 1991.

9. Dieter Ernst and David O'Connor, *Competing in the Electron-*

ics Industry—The Experience of Newly Industrializing Countries (London: Pinter, 1992), p. 37.

10. Congressional Budget Office, *The Benefits and Risks of Federal Funding for Sematech* (Washington, D.C.: Congressional Budget Office, 1987), p. 29.

11. Douglas Irwin and Peter Klenow, "Learning-by-Doing Spillovers in the Semiconductor Industry," *Journal of Political Economy*, vol. 102 (1994), pp. 1200–27.

12. Douglas Irwin, "Trade Politics and the Semiconductor Industry," Paper prepared for the National Bureau of Economic Research conference on the political economy of trade protection, February 3–4, 1994, table 1.

13. Arthur T. Denzau, "Trade Protection Comes to the Valley—Silicon Valley," Mimeo, Center for the Study of American Business, Washington University, June 1988.

14. Brink Lindsey, "DRAM Scam: How the United States Built an Industrial Policy on Sand," *Reason*, February 1992, p. 48.

15. John J. Lazlo, Jr., *The Japanese Semiconductor Industry* (San Francisco: Hambrecht and Quist, 1985), pp. 14–15.

CHAPTER 6: MANAGING SEMICONDUCTOR TRADE

1. See Andrew R. Dick, "Learning by Doing and Dumping in the Semiconductor Industry," *Journal of Law and Economics*, vol. 34, no. 1 (April 1991), pp. 133–59, for a complete discussion and analysis of how competitive learning by doing was confused with anticompetitive dumping in the semiconductor industry.

CHAPTER 7: THE GOVERNMENT CARTEL

1. Irwin, "Trade Politics and the Semiconductor Industry," p. 48.

2. David C. Mowery and Nathan Rosenberg, "New Developments in U.S. Technology Policy: Implications for Competitiveness and International Trade Policy," *California Management Review*, vol. 32, no. 1 (Fall 1989), p. 113.

3. Text of side-letter to the 1986 U.S.-Japan Semiconductor Agreement, published in *Inside U.S. Trade*, vol. 6, no. 46, November 18, 1988.

4. Angel, *Restructuring for Innovation*, p. 179.

5. Ibid., pp. 179–80.

6. Thomas A. Pugel, "Limits of Trade Policy toward High Technology Industries: The Case of Semiconductors," in Ryuzo Sato and Paul Wachtel, eds., *Trade Friction and Economic Policy* (Cambridge: Cambridge University Press, 1987), p. 204.

7. Tyson, *Who's Bashing Whom?* p. 112.

8. Kenneth Flamm, "Making New Rules: High-Tech Trade Friction and the Semiconductor Industry," *Brookings Review*, vol. 9, no. 2 (Spring 1991), p. 28.

9. Eugene Volokh, "The Semiconductor Industry and Foreign Competition," *Cato Institute Policy Analysis*, no. 99, January 28, 1988, p. 23.

10. Tyson, *Who's Bashing Whom?* p. 113.

11. Japan also was accused of shifting some production offshore to avoid the pricing regulations under the agreement. Exports of unassembled chips were subject to FMV prices, but these were lower than those set for fully assembled chips. Further, the "transfer prices" set on unassembled chips exported to offshore assembly affiliates were largely arbitrary.

12. Japan also negotiated an export price floor agreement with the European Community in 1989 that largely mirrored the 1986 agreement with the United States and that was intended to reduce instances of smuggling between Europe and the United States. See Jacob M. Schlesinger, "Japan Chip Makers Reach Agreement with EC on Prices," *Wall Street Journal*, August 21, 1989.

13. Lindsey, "Don't Renew the Semiconductor Cartel."

14. The exceptions were Texas Instruments and Micron Technology.

15. Tyson, *Who's Bashing Whom?* p. 116.

16. Ibid., p. 117.

17. Angel, *Restructuring for Innovation*, p. 182.

18. Irwin, "Trade Politics and the Semiconductor Industry," pp. 65–66.

19. Semiconductor Industry Association, *Four Years of Experience under the U.S.-Japan Semiconductor Agreement: "A Deal Is a Deal"* (Cupertino, Calif.: Semiconductor Industry Association, 1990), p. 33.

20. Lindsey, "DRAM Scam," p. 48.

21. This history is chronicled in Dick, "Learning by Doing and Dumping in the Semiconductor Industry."

22. Irwin, "Trade Politics and the Semiconductor Industry," pp. 67–68.

23. Robert Keatley, "U.S. Duties on Korean Semiconductors Raise Double-Edged Sword to Dumping," *Wall Street Journal,* February 19, 1993.

24. *Inside U.S. Trade,* March 19, 1993, p. 20.

CHAPTER 8: THE SEMATECH EXPERIMENT

1. Peter Grindley, David Mowery, and Brian Silverman, "Sematech and Collaborative Research: Lessons in the Design of High-Technology Consortia," Discussion paper, University of California at Berkeley, August 1993, p. 29.

2. White House Press Office, *Technology for America's Economic Growth: A New Direction to Build Economic Strength,* February 22, 1993.

3. Paul M. Romer, "Implementing a National Technology Strategy with Self-Organizing Investment Boards," *Brookings Papers on Economic Activity: Microeconomics,* vol. 2 (1993), pp. 345–90.

4. U.S. General Accounting Office, *Federal Research: Sematech's Efforts to Strengthen the U.S. Semiconductor Industry,* GAO/RCED-90-236, 1990, p. 11.

5. U.S. Congressional Budget Office, *The Benefits and Risks of Federal Funding for Sematech* (Washington, D.C.: U.S. Congressional Budget Office, 1987).

6. William J. Spencer and Peter Grindley, "Sematech after Five Years: High Technology Consortia and U.S. Competitiveness," *California Management Review* (Summer 1993), p. 16.

7. Angel, *Restructuring for Innovation,* p. 169.

8. Spencer and Grindley, "Sematech after Five Years," p. 15.

9. Grindley, Mowery, and Silverman, "Sematech and Collaborative Research," p. 8.

10. Spencer and Grindley, "Sematech after Five Years," p. 10.

11. Ibid.

12. Lindsey, "DRAM Scam," p. 43.

13. Douglas Irwin and Peter Klenow, "High Tech R&D Subsidies: The Effects of Sematech," Mimeo, University of Chicago, 1994, p. 6.

14. Angel, *Restructuring for Innovation,* p. 174; and "Uncle Sam's Helping Hand," *Economist,* April 2, 1994, p. 24. See also Grindley,

Mowery, and Silverman, "Sematech and Collaborative Research," pp. 19–20.

15. "Uncle Sam's Helping Hand," p. 24.

16. Irwin and Klenow, "High Tech R&D Subsidies."

17. U.S. General Accounting Office, *Federal Research: Sematech's Technological Progress and Proposed R&D Program*, GAO/RCED-92-223BR, 1992.

18. The three firms leaving Sematech were LSI Logic and Micron Technologies (in 1992) and Harris Corporation (in 1993).

19. Irwin and Klenow, "High Tech R&D Subsidies," p. 8.

20. Lindsey, "DRAM Scam," p. 47.

21. Ibid., p. 48.

22. Quoted in "Uncle Sam's Helping Hand," *Economist*, April 2, 1994, p. 24.

23. Lindsey, "DRAM Scam," p. 44. Subsequent efforts to create a chip manufacturing consortium, U.S. Memories, were abandoned when its backers failed to attract either public or sufficient private financial backing; see Stephen K. Yoder, "Lessons Linger As U.S. Memories Fail," *Wall Street Journal*, January 16, 1990.

24. Grindley, Mowery, and Silverman, "Sematech and Collaborative Research."

25. Mowery and Rosenberg, "New Developments in U.S. Technology Policy," p. 118.

CHAPTER 9: LOOKING TO THE FUTURE

1. Tyson, *Who's Bashing Whom?* p. 286.

2. Quoted in Bob Davis and G. Pascal Zachary, "Electronics Firms Get Push from Clinton to Join Industrial Policy Initiative in Flat-Panel Displays," *Wall Street Journal*, April 28, 1994. Kenneth Flamm provides a lengthy defense of the Clinton administration's industrial policy intitiatives in FPDs: "Flat-Panel Displays: Catalyzing a U.S. Industry," *Issues in Science and Technology* (Fall 1994), pp. 27–32. For an opposing viewpoint, see Claude Barfield, "Flat Panel Displays: A Second Look," *Issues in Science and Technology* (Winter 1994–95), pp. 21–25.

3. Barfield, "Flat Panel Displays," p. 22.

4. Bob Davis, "Clinton's Key Technology-Policy Effort Is Dealt a Blow by Congressional Study," *Wall Street Journal*, May 3, 1995.

About the Author

ANDREW R. DICK is an assistant professor of economics at the University of California, Los Angeles. He received his Ph.D. in 1989 from the University of Chicago. He has written widely on international trade policy, industrial organization, and the Japanese economy.